A MONTESSORI HANDBOOK

order, classification, gradation, discrimination

Teacher as a guide.
child teaching other children

ownership, privacy, structure

movement   practice,
*   repetition,*
sensory   reinforcement
intellectual

early, pre-school opportunities

freedom within limitations
opportunity to progress at own pace, when the child is ready

A MONTESSORI HANDBOOK

"Dr. Montessori's Own Handbook"

EDITED BY

R. C. OREM

WITH ADDITIONAL NEW MATERIAL ON CURRENT

MONTESSORI THEORY AND PRACTICE

Capricorn Books
New York

CAPRICORN BOOKS EDITION 1966.
Sixth Impression

Library of Congress Catalog
Card Number 65-25613

PRINTED IN THE UNITED STATES OF AMERICA

To Emmett J. Orem

1881-1965

CONTENTS

7

APPENDICES

Illustrations will be found following page 96

ACKNOWLEDGMENTS

THE EDITOR wishes to acknowledge here his appreciation to the following persons who have, in so many ways, stimulated his interest in early childhood education and encouraged him to seek the man within the child:

Dean Vernon Anderson; Assistant Dean Morris McClure; Dr. Glen Blough; Dr. Kenneth Hovet and Dr. Richard Byrne, University of Maryland College of Education.

Dr. Daniel Prescott; Dr. Madeline Mershon; Dr. Walter Waetjen; Dr. Fred Thompson; Dr. Richard Brandt and Dr. Bernard Peck, Institute for Child Study.

Mr. James Busick, Dorchester County, Md. Board of Education; Mr. Otis Trice, Cambridge High School; Dr. Robert Lamborn, McDonough School; Mr. Quinton Thompson, The Middle School; Mr. William O'Connor, Baltimore College of Commerce.

Sr. Mary Roberta, St. Mary's Dominican College; Mrs. Chandra Fernando, The Lilliput Schoolhouse; Mrs. Marie Fonseca, Manor School; John Blessington, Whitby School; Mrs. Carol Ferguson, Little School House; Mr. and Mrs. Donald Varga, Gloria Dei School; Mr. and Mrs. Ronald Katims, Little Flower Montessori School of New Jersey; Mrs. Gertrude Trent, Seton Montessori School; Mrs. Mae Gadpaille.

Dr. Norris Haring, University of Kansas Medical Center; Dr. Sylvia Richardson, University of Oklahoma Medical Center; Dr. J. McV. Hunt, University of Illinois; Dr. Ronald Koegeler, UCLA; Dr. G. N. Getman, Optometric Extension Program.

Friends and patrons of the Lilliput Schoolhouse; officers and members of the Corpus Christi Montessori Society, the Greater New Orleans Montessori Society, and the Washington Montessori Society.

Miss Winifred Thompson, D.C. Department of Public Welfare; Dr. B. G. Meese, D.C. Children's Center; Mrs. Helen Curley, Director of Nursing; Mr. James Wyatt, Director of Education, Mr. William Barr, Cedar Knoll School, Mr. Guy Puntch, District Training School, Mr. Carl Oliver, Maple Glen School.

Mrs. Cleo Monson, American Montessori Society; Mr. and Mrs. Douglas Gravel.

Mr. and Mrs. Robert Pula; Mr. and Mrs. Robert Seaton; Mr. and Mrs. William Clements; Mr. and Mrs. Robert Shellow; Mr. and Mrs. Robert Rambusch; Mr. and Mrs. Gilbert Donahue; Miss Elizabeth Hall; Miss Kathleen Sperry; Mr. and Mrs. Robert Earley; Dr. and Mrs. Victor Cicirelli; Dr. George Weller; Dr. and Mrs. John Marshall, Mr. and Mrs. Clifford Brothers, Mrs. Wilhelmina Opey.

Mr. Mario M. Montessori, Association Montessori Internationale; Mr. A. M. Joosten, Indian Montessori Training Courses; Miss Betty Stephenson, Washington Montessori Institute.

Mr. Sheridan C. Lewis, Southern Coast Company.

The photographs on pages 1 and 2 of the picture section and the top photographs on pages 13, 15 and 16, are supplied by courtesy of Dr. Hector Oliveira; all other photographs are by Leland E. Lindsay, Corpus Christi, Texas.

INTRODUCTION

The Montessori Method and the Handbook

1

THE MONTESSORI Method is a spontaneous, expansive educational system designed to afford the child liberty to move and act in a prepared environment encouraging self-development.

The first woman to receive a medical degree from the University of Rome, Maria Montessori was, variously, assistant doctor at the University Psychiatric Clinic, Director of the Medical Pedagogical Institute, private physician, and lecturer in anthropology at the University of Rome. The influence of her medical background and a lasting interest in biology are evident in the method and materials associated with her name. Montessori sees the child's physical and psychological development as comprised of distinct phases or "sensitive periods," each with its own needs and subject to the guidance of natural laws of development. The formative period from birth to age six, she says, is most crucial; during this time the child is "constructing" his personality through "experiences on the environment" which should be scaled to his physical needs and responsive to his unique absorbent mentality. It was this unique mentality of the child that actually inspired Montessori to devote her life to the study of childhood learning and made possible the development of her remarkably novel approach to education.

The child as worker, allowed to concentrate upon self-chosen tasks of interest in the freedom of a "Children's House," displays a tremendous capacity for achieving ever-higher levels of independence within a framework of social awareness. In contrast is the child who must cope with the distractions of the random stimuli found in an "unprepared environment." With the development of his self-direction frustrated by constant failure at tasks for which he is ill prepared, such a child often turns against the society that has shown itself insensitive to his needs.

Montessori recognized the importance of such elements as programmed preparation, practice, imitation, and repetition in the young child's learning. She saw that he needs to be in touch with reality through much manual activity involving the manipulation of interesting didactic materials. Her experimentally developed materials, carefully regulated in terms of their quantity and qualities, contain built-in "control of error" making self-correction possible and enabling the user to work much of the time independently at his own pace. Moreover, the teacher is freed to give individual lessons as needed.

Because the child, during his formative period, is capable of absorbing material such as language directly from his environment, the role of the "new teacher," or "directress" as Montessori sometimes refers to her, is to indirectly assist the child's development by preparing and maintaining an optimum environment for him. The teacher, trained in objective observation, becomes the child's interpreter and the defender of his spontaneity, limiting her intervention and verbal behavior as she encourages the child's "auto-education."

Montessori believed that the properties of the child's "mathematical mind" predispose him to organize, classify, and order the information received by his senses, resulting in a prepared or ordered mind necessary for self-mastery and mastery of the environment.

Although it can be said that the young child learns through

movement, traditional education has tended to limit his opportunity to experience actively and directly. Montessori made adequate provision for movement in her method, pointing out that the child is by nature an active learner. Teachers and all adults must be mindful of the child's need to move and be appreciative of his learning potential which is best expressed through work (experiences in an orderly environment).

According to Montessori, the fact that virtually all children suffer trauma during their development dramatizes the need for an "education from birth" based upon a science of child care, including care of the newborn. The child, says Montessori, offers a number of hopes for the future. Her concept of the "new child," the child "believed in but not yet seen," holds that in a new environment, which must include respectful adults, the child will reveal unforeseen potentials for inner motivation and self-discipline leading to new standards of "auto-formation." When we understand the child's power of self-development, we shall better know what the man may become.

The child can be said to link two adult generations or, put somewhat differently, two periods of history. To raise the level of man's functioning, to usher in a new cultural era, the unique learning capacities of childhood must be utilized. It is in the child, not the adult, that Montessori sees the hope for the emergence of a new mankind tantamount to a new race of "spiritual men," capable of achieving a new plane of ethics to which man already strives, however falteringly. The potential, then, for a "new man" is in the child, whose development in all spheres—physical, emotional, intellectual, social, and spiritual—needs safeguarding and the optimum nourishment made possible in a "prepared environment." Seen in this light, Montessori's "Children's House" becomes the model for a much-needed reformation of the environment at large.

2

Described by Montessori as "the only authentic manual of the Montessori Method," *Dr. Montessori's Own Handbook* has served for more than fifty years as a concise guide to the method and materials now identified with her name throughout the world. Originally published in 1914, two years after her best seller, *The Montessori Method,* had appeared in English, the *Handbook* contains the pedagogical essence of that earlier classic, but in one-third the number of pages. The *Handbook* is her masterpiece in miniature.

This modern edition, at the heart of which is the text of the 1914 book, provides much new explanatory material, with new illustrations, all arranged in a more functional format than the earlier work. Featured are contemporary statements by ten contributors, including the editor, that deal directly or indirectly with Montessori principles and procedures.

The contributors are a diverse group: a physician, an optometrist, a psychologist, a special education foundation director, a university educator, a government administrator, an institutional staff training officer, a professional artist, a reading consultant, and a Montessori headmistress. Six hold doctorates in their fields, and three have children in Montessori schools.

The original *Handbook* text has been divided into five sections, each covering several related topics. The passages from Montessori are preceded by helpful summaries that relate her statements to modern practice and to the statements of other educational theorists.

Section I: The Montessori Structure

This section contains an outline of the methods and materials used in a "Children's House," and a discussion of Montessori's views on the all-important role of freedom in education. The milieu of the "prepared environment" provides what could be described as a "pocket of order" within which children may benefit developmentally from the security of an environmental consistency altogether too rare in their larger surroundings. Montessori children have an interesting, carefully graded array of tasks from which to choose, and are permitted as much practice and repetition as they need to master these tasks; moreover, they are free to proceed at their own pace uninterrupted.

Sections II, III, and IV cover the key principles of Montessori's three-pronged educational approach: motor, sensory, and intellectual. In both her *Method* and *Handbook* she follows this sequence, acknowledging that the child must first gain a large measure of confidence in his body's motor capacities before moving to sensory competence and then to intellectual conquest. Lauretta Bender has likewise noted that a preliminary step to all education is "the motor education of every child."[1]

Section II: The Importance of Movement in Education

In this section Montessori describes the highlights of a program for motor or muscular education to serve as the base for the child's other learnings. Her interest in providing school children adequate nourishment and exercise in healthful surroundings foreshadows by half a century contemporary concern for the physical fitness of American youth.

D. B. Harmon, G. N. Getman and other researchers are currently synthesizing knowledge from the fields of architecture, education, engineering, medicine, psychology, and vision to construct an "educational anthropology" in which training in bodily rhythm and coordination and form perception furnishes a foundation for formal learning. Their research indicates that virtually all first-graders taught conventionally do not achieve up to their capacities.[2] Dr. Getman refers to "the extensive work of Montessori" in his little volume, *How to Develop Your Child's Intelligence*.[3]

Section III: Sensory Education and Music

This section contains detailed material reflecting the significance Montessori accords to the sense training phase of her method. She believes all the senses should be systematically prepared and then utilized in the service of learning. Montessori's sensorial material is another example of the means by which she gives the child learning opportunities that would otherwise be typically unavailable.

Educators currently struggling to combat the profound effects of cultural deprivation upon hundreds of thousands of urban (and rural) children could well study the pioneer endeavors in this field by the great Italian physician-educator, who opened her first *Casa dei Bambini* in a Roman slum tenement. America's big educational gun in the "war on poverty" may prove to be the structured setting for preschoolers conceived and developed by Montessori.

The didactic material of the prepared environment comprises, in effect, a splendid toolbox for learning, from which the child is free to select whatever is necessary for his work of self-development. Montessori's discussion of sensory education leads to the subject of music, which is briefly treated.

Section IV: Intellectual Education

In this section is outlined Montessori's multisensory "programmed" approach to the pedagogy of language and arithmetic, employing interesting, sequential didactic material. Grace Fernald has noted, in *Remedial Techniques in Basic School Subjects*, that the effectiveness of the Montessori Method in the development of letter and word forms "cannot be questioned by anyone who has seen a good Montessori school in operation."[4]

Section V: A New Child—A New Man

The development of self-discipline in Montessori classes is reviewed in this section, which concludes with a plea for the implementation of a new education to match the needs of the twentieth-century child. Such a truly child-centered education could free the unrealized potential of humans to function more creatively as individuals and more harmoniously as members of society.

R. C. OREM

Selected References

[1] Bender, Lauretta, *Psychopathology of Children with Brain Disorders.* Springfield, Illinois: Charles Thomas, 1956. P. 25.

[2] Rice, Arthur, "Rhythmic Training and Body Balancing Prepare Child for Formal Learning." *The Nation's Schools,* February, 1962.

[3] Getman, G. N., *How to Develop Your Child's Intelligence.* Luverne, Minnesota: Dr. G. N. Getman, 1958. P. 19.

[4] Fernald, Grace, *Remedial Techniques in Basic School Subjects.* New York: McGraw-Hill, 1943. P. 29.

PREFACE

IF a preface is a light which should serve to illumine the contents of a volume, I choose, not words, but human figures to illustrate this little book intended to enter families where children are growing up. I therefore recall here, as an eloquent symbol, Helen Keller and Mrs. Anne Sullivan Macy, who are, by their example, both teachers to myself—and, before the world, living documents of the miracle in education.

In fact, Helen Keller is a marvelous example of the phenomenon common to all human beings: the possibility of the liberation of the imprisoned spirit of man by the education of the senses. Here lies the basis of the method of education of which the book gives a succinct idea.

If one only of the senses sufficed to make of Helen Keller a woman of exceptional culture and a writer, who better than she proves the potency of that method of education which builds on the senses? If Helen Keller attained through exquisite natural gifts to an elevated conception of the world, who better than she proves that in the inmost self of man lies the spirit ready to reveal itself?

Helen, clasp to your heart these little children, since they, above all others, will understand you. They are your younger brothers, when, with blindfolded eyes and in silence, they touch with their little hands, profound impressions rise in their consciousness, and they exclaim with a new form of happiness: "I see with my hands." They alone, then, can fully understand the drama of the mysterious privilege your soul has known. When, in darkness and in silence, their spirit left free to expand, their intellectual energy redoubled, they become able to read and write without having learned, almost as it were by intuition, they, only they, can understand in part the ecstasy which God granted you on the luminous path of learning.

MARIA MONTESSORI.

Throughout her Handbook, *Montessori reiterates the importance of the tactile sense and manual activity in education. Researcher Earl Alluisi notes that "man is tactually literate," giving Helen Keller as perhaps the most remarkable case in point. She not only reads with her fingers and writes with her fingers by typewriter, but also "listens" with the skin of her hands and "speaks" with her fingertips.*[1]

Selected References

[1] Alluisi, Earl, "Toward Optimizing Man's Tactile Communication." *Perceptual and Motor Skills,* 12, 1961, pp. 235-245.

NOTE BY THE AUTHOR

As a result of the widespread interest that has been taken in my method of child education, certain books have been issued which may appear to the general reader to be authoritative expositions of the Montessori system. I wish to state definitely that the present work, the English translation of which has been authorized and approved by me, is the only authentic manual of the Montessori method, and that the only other authentic or authorized works of mine in the English language are *The Montessori Method,* and *Pedagogical Anthropology.*

Maria Montessori

I

THE MONTESSORI STRUCTURE

If it were necessary to compress the description of the principles of the Montessori method into a single phrase, perhaps the most comprehensive would be that it was a method based on "Liberty in a Prepared Environment."

—*The Child in the Church*, p. 110*

---

* The quotations used as section headings throughout this book have been selected from Dr. Montessori's numerous other writings.

Montessori Perspectives,
Past and Present

NEARLY sixty years ago, a young Italian woman doctor named Maria Montessori opened a small experimental school in a poor neighborhood in the San Lorenzo district of Rome. Although, at the time, the event received only limited notice, today it is recognized as a turning point in educational theory and practice. By the mid-1960's there were hundreds of schools throughout the Western world patterned on that original experiment; and, though the United States lagged behind the Continent in the development of Montessori schools, by 1965 there were some 200 in operation in this country, with the figure increasing rapidly.

Maria Montessori became interested in education while working with defective children in a psychiatric clinic. Out of her extensive experience in the clinic and in various other educational settings, she devised a new approach to the education of normal children. The original *Casa dei Bambini* ("Children's House") was started in the first decade of this century to test this approach. From the vantage point of current research in the psychology of learning we are able to assert that the educational theory and materials of Montessori constitute a remarkable break with traditional pedagogical practices. Maria Montessori, by combining liberty with the "organization of work," was the first educational innovator to basically alter in concept and in method the timing and format of Western educational practices.

Roots of education in the West can be traced back at least

some 4,000 years, to the Egyptians, who taught reading, writing, and arithmetic. From that time to this, the format of the classroom has usually been to assemble a group of students before the teacher who then instructs by lecture and demonstration. If the students do not attend to the lecture or master the lesson, they are punished. In this situation only the teacher is active, free to talk and move. The students are compelled to be quiet and still in a condition supposed, then as now, to be ideal for the absorption of knowledge.

After four thousand years of education, the design of the classroom remains much the same; and though there have been changes and improvements in subject matter, the methods of presentation have also remained essentially the same. The only educational theorist to successfully alter this arrangement, in actual practice, was Maria Montessori. She broke the rigid pattern of the conventional classroom and provided the child with freedom of movement and expression. In a Montessori class each child is given a personal space and permitted to move about and talk.

This basic concern with freedom indicates the liberal character of Montessori's thought. She was a product of the nineteenth-century liberal tradition, with its social reform. Throughout the Western world in the 1800's the common man was asserting his right to political and economic freedom. Montessori saw clearly that the social reforms should apply to the child as well as the adult. If the adult was to have dignity, freedom and opportunity to develop his individual potentials, then so should the child. The Montessori classroom provided the child the same individualism and freedom that political reformers advocated for society in general.

Maria Montessori was quite conscious of this parallel. In one place, discussing the reforms in Europe which had followed the French Revolution, she writes:

The poor have not yet had proper consideration, and always there remains one class that is yet more completely ignored, even among the rich. Such is childhood! All social problems are considered from the point of view of the adult and his needs. . . . Far more important are the needs of the child.[1]

In the Montessori social philosophy the child is seen as a class member, much as the worker, farmer, or landowner had been in classical economic theory. Later in the same essay she comments:

Suppose we set up in schools the same social improvements that we are so proud of achieving! Let us feed the children, give them playgrounds, clothing, freedom of speech.[2]

In a very real sense, the Montessori Method is a Declaration of Independence for the child.

This emphasis on freedom reminds one immediately of the progressive educational movement that experimented with complete freedom for the child in the classroom. This movement, which ran its course during the first half of the twentieth century in the United States, probably produced more chaos than education. However, it is important to note that the Montessori Method is basically different from the extremes of the progressive method. Montessori was never in favor of absolute freedom for the child. She believed that freedom must exist within limits. Her educational theory created an environment in which the historical experience of Western society was dominant, and in which the child's freedom was limited to a choice as to which aspect of our culture he would master first.

Montessori did not believe that the child could be counted upon to reproduce the several thousand years of accumulated ideas and technology that make up our tradition. She recognized that the very young child is imitative as well as creative. The genius of the child is his amazing ability to reproduce faithfully the cultural forms to which he has been exposed. Montessori attempted to create a classroom in which the child would first have an opportunity to reproduce the patterns of culture that surround him, by utilizing his unique absorptive mentality.

On the other hand, she recognized that education must be more than the mere imposition of values and techniques upon the younger generation. The primitive educational institutions that have dominated education throughout history inflict on the child a rigid scheme of behavior in which he is compelled to make the desired responses or suffer punishment. And while today the rod is largely abandoned, its function, coercion, has not been eliminated, but only replaced by more subtle teacher tactics. The contemporary schoolmaster has too often become a master of the art of psychological compulsion. Anxiety and fear can be at least as effective as physical pain in controlling behavior.

Montessori rejected the use of such damaging controls. She recognized that anxiety, fear, and pain inhibit the drive for exploration and appetite for curiosity. In this she anticipated the findings of one of the leading learning theorists of our own period. B. F. Skinner, the Harvard psychologist, has written that aversion from fear or anxiety is a major cause of learning disability. Skinner believes that we literally teach our children to resist learning.

> The child at his desk, filling in his workbook, is behaving primarily to escape from the threat of a series of minor aversive events—the teacher's displeasure, the criticism or ridicule of his classmates, an ignominious showing in a competition, low marks, a trip to the office "to be talked to" by the principal, or a word to the parent who may still resort to the birch rod. In this welter of aversive consequences, getting the right answer is in itself an insignificant event.[3]

The central concern of the Montessori educational method is to create a learning environment in which the child can acquire the "tools" of his culture without losing his sense of initiative. She recognized that academic accomplishment should never be realized through means which break the spirit of the learner. At the root of the Montessori Method is an optimism about man and his nature. Montessori believed that children, if given the opportunity, would strive to master their environment. Education did not, she felt, have to be imposed on the child. If we would only respect the natural impulse of the child to explore his surroundings and to organize his experience, he could be led into a mastery of his culture.

In the Montessori class, the child is surrounded by a variety of educational devices all carefully designed to appeal to the mind of a *child*. He is given the freedom of choice to select any of a wide range of didactic materials that appeal to him. These materials are actually "learning games" serving as avenues into our cultural heritage. Montessori students are initiated into a nondirective learning situation within which they are channeled into activities leading to a mastery of the three dominant symbol systems of human society: reading, writing and mathematics.

The Montessori Method represents a dynamic balance between the extremes of progressive and traditional educational philosophy. On the one hand she accommodates the child's freedom and individualism; on the other, she insures that the essential skills of the heritage will be accurately transmitted to the next generation. Montessori regarded the school as an institution of learning and not as an agency of social adjustment. Her concept of freedom meant freedom to choose between alternatives carefully structured into the learning situation. In order to see this it is necessary to describe the Montessori classroom in somewhat more detail.

In an ideal Montessori school, education begins at about three. The child is brought into a social environment of children involving an age span of some three years. In a typical class, for example, one might find three-, four-, and five-year-old children. Each child has his own working area with a table, chair, and rug. This area is his in a most particular sense. His individuality, even at this infant stage, is respected. No other child may enter his working area without his permission.

This simple rule seems obvious once stated, but how many nursery schools make any attempt to protect the private activities of the child from the rampages of other children? For, in fact, is not the conventional nursery school really a thinly disguised baby-care center where order is preserved only in the most general way, with no real effort made to insure that a curious child, working quietly on some task, will be protected from the casual, and sometimes destructive, curiosity of his neighbors?

In the Montessori environment, any child who wishes to work alone for some time may do so in his own area, and the teacher will make a point of protecting his separateness. Any child who disturbs the solitary worker will be gently but firmly shunted off. However, if two or more children wish to work together, they are free to do so. There is no fixed order of activity in the Montessori class.

The "private space" of the individual child sets the tone of the whole environment. The other rules follow from this fundamental concept. The child is told that he may move about at will; the entire room and adjacent areas are open for his investigation with only the reservation discussed above. Moreover, in the Montessori classroom the child is free to talk as much as he wishes. This freedom of movement and expression is not unlimited. The child may not run, shout, or push. Montessori understood the need for order in the classroom; in her method, the freedom of the individual is not absolute. Freedom exists in relation to, and is limited by, the rights of others.

The last ground rule to be discussed governs the learning materials and activities, and parallels those already mentioned. In the classroom the walls are lined with shelves and the shelves contain learning games designed to interest and educate even very young children. The child may take any one of these games not in use and work with it as long as he likes. However, when he is through with the device, it must be replaced in the same condition in which it was found. After the child has selected a game, he may receive instructions from the teacher and assistance from other children when he wishes it. He may also help another child. The four-year-old may be seen helping the three-year-old on a particular task, while receiving help later from a five-year-old on another task.

There are rules for the teacher also, and the most basic of these echoes the general philosophy of the Montessori Method. As the child is introduced into the learning environment, the teacher explains and enforces the rules which govern the little world of the "prepared environment." She shows the child the many learning games that line the shelves and makes it clear that he may take any which interest him, and that she will assist him in mastering their complexities. But, and this is most basic to the system, she must never force the child to begin learning. *The first movement of exploration must come from the child.*

Volition is a characteristic most highly prized in the Montessori classroom. Unlike our contemporary educational institutions, in the Montessori school education is never imposed on the child. It is assumed that the normal child is curious and exploratory and that if he is given an opportunity to establish his own point of contact with his culture, he will begin to learn skills through spontaneous experimentation and imitation—much as the normal child masters his native tongue. Therefore, the teacher must introduce the child into the special environment but never force an activity on him. However, once the child has indicated an interest in an activity, the teacher may provide all the guidance necessary to get the child started.

At this point in our discussion, the Montessori school setting might seem to some to be permissive if not random.

The child's individuality is respected; he is free to choose or not from his environment. But what guarantee do we have that he will choose correctly? It is all very well to speak of freedom and individualism, but education, by its nature, involves an organized presentation of subject matter. Where is the structure and content in the Montessori Method?

Montessori understood that the young child is in many ways a limited creature. Whatever his individual potential, his first task must be to master the tools, values, and concepts of his culture. The child should have freedom, but he must also learn to read and write. Montessori never regarded the child as a special creature born with the innate capacity to transcend his culture by self-expression and self-assertion. She recognized, though many progressive educators have not, that the child must serve an apprenticeship. Therefore, while the Montessori classroom respects the child's freedom, it does not hesitate to channel that freedom by means of nondirective techniques.

When the child enters a Montessori school he finds himself in a world that reflects in miniature the larger world which he will someday occupy. All of the elements in the room are real, functional, and often breakable, but all are scaled down to a level of size and difficulty which enable the child to experiment with them within the framework of his own powers. The tasks that challenge him are carefully broken down into small steps, each of which leads to the next.

The step-by-step design of the Montessori educational apparatus is particularly interesting, for it closely parallels the self-reinforcing, auto-instructional teaching machines of Pressey and Skinner. Montessori anticipated by some fifty years the latest concepts of learning theory. While in this electronic age some of her learning games could be revised and improved, leading learning theorists admit that she was in concept much ahead of her time.

The tables and chairs in the Montessori class are small, but the letters of the alphabet with which the child plays are large. The physical components of the room match the child's small frame, but the symbolic devices are magnified to assist his immature and inexperienced senses. The subjects he must master are presented in large, simple and clear form, while the responses he must make to master them are small and deliberately graded.

Yet, for all this respect for the child's individualism, the content of this environment in which he operates so freely is well structured. The freedom of choice that the Montessori system offers the child is really only the freedom to select which symbol system he will master first. While the classroom permits the child to do whatever he likes, it offers only educational experiences that our society and culture feel to be important. All of the learning games lead the child into a mastery of reading, writing, arithmetic, and related skills.

The freedom is psychological but not intellectual. Montessori never assumed that the young child, left to his own devices with no direction, would reproduce or improve on his culture. The notion, still popular in some quarters, that the child provided with a ball of clay and pot of paint can create masterpieces never occurred to the Italian doctor. She structured the educational process and limited the random exploratory behavior by restricting his choices.

Though in the space of these few pages it is not possible to describe in detail the learning games, a few examples will suffice to demonstrate their character. In the classroom, a child wanders over to a shelf and picks up a puzzle to play with. The puzzle, in color, is perhaps the map of Europe or Asia, leading the child into geography. Or he may select some blocks to work with. They fit together so as to illustrate a mathematical principle which, as the child builds, the teacher will quietly point out. If the child wishes to handle beads, he may do so, but in the process he will be exposed to concepts of number and quantity. There are countless aspects of the Montessori classroom which "lure" the child into our culture and technology.

There is another aspect of educational methodology concerning which the Italian doctor had revolutionary ideas. This is the matter of discipline. Discipline is a problem facing all teachers. How should students' activities be regulated? What acts should be tolerated and which condemned? How does the teacher distinguish between creativity, eccentricity, and destructiveness?

Dr. Montessori was very interested in these questions, and she expressed her views in her writings and classroom practices. First of all, there must be a basic order that protects the individual from the unwanted attentions of his peers. This need for the child to have a private world of action and space has already been mentioned. Mutual respect for the space and actions of others is a requisite of the Montessori learning method. The teacher is required to enforce this order without exception or apology. The child is allowed to walk and talk at will, to work alone or with others, but never to interrupt or interfere by his uninvited acts with the business of others. The rules are the ground for the Montessori concept of discipline.

Beyond this basic preservation of order, a kind of social homeostasis, Montessori recognized a higher level of discipline, which emerges when the individual voluntarily engages in interesting activity. One only has to witness children playing a game in a park or vacant lot. Even though completely unsupervised by adults, the game may proceed for an hour or more in an orderly organized manner.

The discipline that Montessori wished to develop is illustrated by the lives of all creative people. When human energy is in focus it is always disciplined; yet the source of the control is always intrinsic. The height of freedom is the product of discipline illustrated by the free and easy movements of the dancer or the flashing hands of the great pianist.

Freedom is the control that the individual has achieved by the mastery of himself and his environment. Greatness never results from a situation in which the individual is dominated by the environment. All too frequently, Montessori saw children and adults conforming rigidly out of anxiety about the expectations of others. She saw in this the death of the spirit. In *The Montessori Method* she writes:

> Discipline must come through liberty. Here is a great principle which is difficult for followers of common-school methods to understand. How shall one obtain discipline in a class of free children? Certainly in our system, we have a concept of discipline very different from that commonly accepted. If discipline is founded upon liberty, the discipline itself must necessarily be active. We do not consider an individual disciplined only when he has been rendered as artificially silent as a mute and as immovable as a paralytic. He is an individual annihilated, not disciplined.
>
> We call an individual disciplined when he is master of himself, and can, therefore, regulate his own conduct when it shall be necessary to follow some rule of life. Such a concept of active discipline is not easy either to comprehend or to apply. But certainly it contains a great educational principle, very different from the oldtime absolute and undiscussed coercion to immobility.[4]

Montessori had great faith in the energy and uniqueness of the individual; and, within an ordered environment, she wanted to "turn him loose" on the cultural implements of our tradition, for she believed that true discipline is self-discipline. And in the ideal Montessori classroom order is a product of interest. The active learner is orderly and productive by virtue of his personal concern with exploring his own power and the world.

That there is at present a wave of interest in the educational theory and practice of Dr. Maria Montessori is by no means accidental. There are two very compelling reasons for the renaissance of her work in the United States. First, and most consequential, is the research in learning theory that American psychologists have produced in the past few decades. Second is the intelligence, energy and dedication of one woman, Nancy McCormick Rambusch, who, after traveling to England and studying the methods of Dr. Montessori, pioneered the opening of the first of the new Montessori schools in this country.

In opening this school in Connecticut, Mrs. Rambusch was reflecting accurately a new direction in educational theory which has been emerging in the United States. American psychologists have reached the stage in their deliberate investigation of learning theory at which they are ready to make definite and perhaps even definitive statements about child development. Their experimentation has moved beyond the "rat research" which has characterized much of the efforts of recent decades. Having worked their way up the animal kingdom, the students of human behavior are presently rediscovering the work of Montessori. Now, after more than fifty years, the evidence to support her insights is forthcoming.

If there is one prime area that indicates the character of the rebirth of interest in the educational theory and methods of Dr. Montessori, it is the present concern for fully utilizing the child's unique potential for learning between birth and age six. Montessori is the outstanding modern advocate of the importance of early learning. She regarded the period of early childhood as critical in determining the intellectual development of the child. And though, at the time she enunciated her ideas, she had to largely rely upon her own observations for support, subsequent research in several related fields has shown her to be correct.

GEORGE L. STEVENS, M.A.

Selected References

[1] Montessori, Maria, *To Educate the Human Potential*. Adyar, Madras 20, India: Kalakshetra Publications, 1961. P. 120.
[2] *Ibid.*, p. 121.

[3] Skinner, B. F., in *Programmed Learning: Theory and Research*. Edited by Wendell Smith and J. William Moore. Princeton, New Jersey: D. Van Nostrand Co., Inc., 1962. P. 24.

[4] Montessori, Maria, *The Montessori Method*. New York: Frederick Stokes, 1912. P. 86.

A "CHILDREN'S HOUSE"

We offer a very simple suggestion: give the child an environment in which everything is constructed in proportion to himself, and let him live therein.

—*Spontaneous Activity in Education*, p. 19

The first Casa dei Bambini *or "Children's House" was opened on January 6, 1907, in a tenement house in the San Lorenzo slum district of Rome. The subsequent success of Montessori schools in Europe, North and South America, the Far East and other parts of the world attests to the validity of Dr. Montessori's approach to early childhood education. The principles underlying her methodology are applicable to children of varied nationality, religion, socioeconomic status, and mental endowment.*

In this section, some features of a "Children's House" are given. Brief as the description is, it clearly illustrates Montessori's pedagogical genius. Note how she subtly programs the opportunity for rich sensory experience into the child's surroundings. It is no accident, for example, that the tables are of various sizes and geometric shapes, or that color serves an educational as well as an aesthetic function.

She "maximizes a situation educationally," as with the furniture, which is light, so that the children can arrange it, scaled to their physiques, and designed to be washed by the children with soap and water. She repeatedly refers to the importance of proper level in a prepared environment—

clothing hooks within easy reach of the children, low cupboards, children at work on the floor, *etc.*

Individual development is provided for within a framework of group cooperation. For example, the didactic material is the property of all the children, but each child has his own drawer in which to put personal belongings. The child learns self-direction while respecting the rights of others.

The "exercises of practical life," as Montessori referred to them, involve the child's care of himself (such as dressing and grooming), and his care of the environment (such as housecleaning). These activities enable the child to better know and gain mastery of himself and his world.

Other aspects of the prepared environment include the provisions for order, *the opportunity for* individual *movement and activity, and the utilization of nature educationally (garden outside, plants inside, care of pets, etc.). One of the most important elements in the Montessori learning situation is* order. *Children need the security of finding things in the place and condition in which they originally found them.*

Inasmuch as there will be a great deal of didactic material in a Montessori classroom for language, geography, mathematics and other subjects, as well as material for sensory education and the exercises of practical life (which are, as already noted, essentially household and grooming activities), the teacher must decide before starting the class where she will place everything, and she should make few if any changes as the year progresses.

Dr. J. McV. Hunt, author of Intelligence and Experience,[1] *and speaker at the 1964 national Montessori seminar in Washington, D.C., calls for a better match between the young child's environment and his potential for intellectual development. Hunt has drawn upon the work of Jean Piaget, the Swiss psychologist who perhaps more than any other contemporary scientist is responsible for developing a methodology for exploring the young child's thinking. In the*

UNESCO publication Education and Mental Health, *reference is made to the Montessori type of activity pursued by Piaget's subjects.*[2]

Selected References

[1] Hunt, Joseph McV., *Intelligence and Experience*. New York: Ronald, 1961.

[2] Wall, W. D., *Education and Mental Health*. Place de Fontenoy, Paris 7e: UNESCO, 1955. P. 61.

A "Children's House"

The "Children's House" is the *environment* which is offered to the child that he may be given the opportunity of developing his activities. This kind of school is not of a fixed type, but may vary according to the financial resources available and to the opportunities afforded by the environment. It ought to be a real house; that is to say, a set of rooms with a garden of which the children are the masters. A garden which contains shelters is ideal, because the children can play or sleep under them, and can also bring their tables out to work or dine. In this way they may live almost entirely in the open air, and are protected at the same time from rain and sun.

The central and principal room of the building, often also the only room at the disposal of the children, is the room for "intellectual work." To this central room can be added other smaller rooms according to the means and opportunities of the place: for example, a bathroom, a dining room, a little parlor or common room, a room for manual work, a gymnasium and rest room.

The special characteristic of the equipment of these houses is that it is adapted for children and not adults. They contain not only didactic material specially fitted for the intellectual development of the child, but also a complete equipment for the management of the miniature family. The furniture is light so that the children can move it about, and it is painted in some light color so that the children can wash it with soap and water. There are low tables of various sizes and shapes—square, rectangular and round, large and small. The rectangular shape is the most common as two or more children can work at it together. The seats are small wooden chairs, but there are also small wicker armchairs and sofas.

In the working-room there are two indispensable pieces of furniture. One of these is a very long cupboard with large doors. It is very low so that a small child can set on the top of it small objects such as mats, flowers, etc. Inside this cupboard is kept the didactic material which is the common property of all the children.

The other is a chest of drawers containing two or three columns of little drawers, each of which has a bright handle (or a handle of some color to contrast with the background), and a small card with a name upon it. Every child has his own drawer, in which to put things belonging to him.

Round the walls of the room are fixed blackboards at a low level, so that the children can write or draw on them, and pleasing, artistic pictures, which are changed from time to time as circumstances direct. The pictures represent children, families, landscapes, flowers and fruit, and more often Biblical and historical incidents. Ornamental plants and flowering plants ought always to be placed in the room where the children are at work.

Another part of the working room's equipment is seen in the pieces of carpet of various colors—red, blue, pink, green and brown. The children spread these rugs upon the floor, sit upon them and work there with the didactic material. A room of this kind is larger than the customary classrooms, not only because the little tables and separate chairs take up more space, but also because a large part of the floor must be free for the children to spread their rugs and work upon them.

In the sitting room, or "club room," a kind of parlor in which the children amuse themselves by conversation, games, or music, etc., the furnishings should be especially tasteful. Little tables of different sizes, little armchairs and sofas should be placed here and there. Many brackets of all kinds and sizes, upon which may be put statuettes, artistic vases or framed photographs, should adorn the walls; and, above all, each child should have a little flowerpot, in which he may sow the seed of some indoor plant, to tend and cultivate it as it grows. On the tables of this sitting room should be placed large albums of colored pictures, and also games of patience, or various geometric solids, with which the children can play at pleasure, constructing figures, etc. A piano, or, better, other musical instruments, possibly harps of small dimensions, made especially for children, completes the equipment. In this "club room" the teacher may sometimes entertain the children with stories, which will attract a circle of interested listeners.

The furniture of the dining room consists, in addition to the tables, of low cupboards accessible to all the children, who can themselves put in their place and take away the crockery, spoons, knives and forks, tablecloth and napkins. The plates are always of china, and the tumblers and water bottles of glass. Knives are always included in the table equipment.

The Dressing Room. Here each child has his own little cupboard or shelf. In the middle of the room there are very simple washstands, consisting of tables, on each of which stand a small basin, soap and nailbrush. Against the wall stand little sinks with water taps. Here the children may draw and pour away their water. There is no limit to the equipment of the "Children's Houses" because the children themselves do everything. They sweep the rooms, dust and wash the furniture, polish the brasses, lay and clear away the table, wash up, sweep and roll up the rugs, wash a few little clothes, and cook eggs. As regards their personal toilet, the children know how to dress and undress themselves. They hang their clothes on little hooks, placed very low so as to be within reach of a little child, or else they fold up such articles of clothing, as their little serving aprons, of which they take great care, and lay them inside a cupboard kept for the household linen.

In short, where the manufacture of toys has been brought to such a point of complication and perfection that children have at their disposal entire dolls' houses, complete wardrobes for the dressing and undressing of dolls, kitchens where they can pretend to cook, toy animals as nearly lifelike as possible, this method seeks to give all this to the child in reality—making him an actor in a living scene.

OUTLINE OF METHOD AND MATERIALS

> The method used by me is that of making a pedagogical experiment with a didactic object and awaiting the spontaneous reaction of the child.
>
> —*The Montessori Method*, p. 167

Montessori developed an elaborate set of "didactic" or teaching materials that provide the child with what could be termed "perceptual basic training." These objects and devices, made of wood, metal, cloth, cardboard, and other materials, are designed to give the child orderly exposure to number, color, texture, weight, sound, and other dimensions of sensory experience. This training serves as preparation for reading, writing, arithmetic, geometry, and other "tool subjects."

To appreciate the many features built into the "didactic" material, or "didactic apparatus" as it is sometimes called, the reader should arrange to see it, preferably in the hands of children. Montessori drew inspiration and ideas for this material from many sources: her own invention, modifications of the objects of other educators, her teachers, the children themselves.

Montessori's emphasis on the importance of early learning and the development of the child before six contrasts with our culture's general neglect of the preschooler's potential as a learner. In some states, for example, the institution of the kindergarten (for five-year-olds) does not even come under the aegis of public education but, rather, under that of the Department of Welfare. The education of three- and four-year-olds is taken even less seriously.

And yet, the young child's experiences will exert a lasting and pervasive influence on later behavior.

We have mistakenly tended to think of the child's education as properly beginning at age six, and also have placed too much confidence in his ability to learn from verbal stimuli. The child, long before six, should be helped to learn how to focus his attention, to carry a task through to successful completion, to become competent as an emergent learner. It is perhaps less a question of content than of an approach orienting children toward learning how to learn, establishing "directional sets" which will enable youngsters to later master all manner of cultural demands. Much of the "content" should be sensorimotor rather than verbal, and the motivation should be intrinsic instead of extrinsic. For the child, learning is its own reward.

Psychologist William Fowler, who taught his own daughter to read, has reviewed the research concerning learning in infancy and early childhood. His survey shows this to be a neglected but promising field. The limited research that *has been done demonstrates that early training may positively influence a child's performance in many areas of learning. Describing Montessori's remarkable work in the early 1900's as "possibly the last major institutional effort to include a cognitive emphasis at the preschool level," he refers to her successful combination of "the new, child-centered principles with the ancient subject-matter orientation."[1]*

With modified electric typewriters and other devices developed by Dr. Omar K. Moore and his colleagues, children as young as three can learn language skills (reading, writing, etc.) which lead to higher-order symbolic activities such as publishing a little newspaper. In Moore's "responsive environment," the child is allowed to explore at his own pace, free of extrinsic prizes and punishment, with adult intervention kept to a minimum. The child is encouraged to use his own initiative to make discoveries, using Moore's multisensory ("talking typewriters," painted keys and fingertips, etc.) sequential approach to learning.[2]

Moore has been quoted to the effect that, if he had a certain sum of money to spend on twenty Ph.D. candidates and twenty nursery school children, he would spend most of it on the youngest children, "who need it most."[3] Interestingly, Professor Moore speaks of the learning format with which he is experimenting as "autotelic activity" in a "responsive environment," while Montessori uses the nomenclature "auto-education" in a "prepared environment."

Lawrence K. Frank has proposed that the school, supported by the family, be regarded as "our chief agent for cultural renewal." Beginning in nursery school, children should be provided with the materials and learning experience needed to master our new scientific concepts and ways of thinking. He speaks of the importance of what he terms "initial learning," when the child should be "learning how to learn," and mentions Montessori's physical materials and models as "offering possibilities for all children."[4]

Selected References

[1] Fowler, William, "Cognitive Learning in Infancy and Early Childhood." *Psychological Bulletin,* Vol. 59, No. 2, March, 1962, pp. 129-130.

[2] Moore, Omar K., *Autotelic Responsive Environments and Exceptional Children.* 20 Augur St., Hamden, Connecticut: Responsive Environments, Inc., 1963.

[3] Pines, Maya, "How Three-year-olds Teach Themselves to Read—and Love It." *Harper's Magazine,* Vol. 226, No. 1356, p. 61.

[4] Frank, Lawrence K., *The School as Agent for Cultural Renewal.* Cambridge, Massachusetts: Harvard University Press, 1959.

Outline of Method and Materials

The technique of my method as it follows the guidance of the natural physiological and psychological development of the child, may be divided into three parts:

Motor education.

Sensory education.

Language, or intellectual education.

The care and management of the environment itself afford the principal means of motor education, while sensory education and the education of language are provided for by my didactic material.

The didactic material for the *education of the senses* consists of:

(a) Three sets of solid insets.

(b) Three sets of solids in graduated sizes, comprising:
   (1) Pink cubes.
   (2) Brown prisms.
   (3) Rods: (a) colored green; (b) colored alternately red and blue.

(c) Various geometric solids (prism, pyramid, sphere, cylinder, cone, etc.).

(d) Rectangular tablets with rough and smooth surfaces.

(e) A collection of various materials (silk, etc.).

(f) Small wooden tablets of different weights.

(g) Two boxes, each containing sixty-four colored tablets.

(h) A chest of drawers containing plane insets.

(i) Three series of cards on which are pasted geometrical forms in paper.

(k) A collection of cylindrical closed boxes (sounds).

(l) A double series of musical bells, wooden boards on which are painted the lines used in music, small wooden discs for the notes.

Didactic Material for the Preparation for Writing and Arithmetic

(m) Two sloping desks and various iron insets.

(n) Cards on which are pasted sandpaper letters.

(o) Two alphabets of colored cardboard and of different sizes.

(p) A series of cards on which are pasted sandpaper figures (1, 2, 3, etc.).

(q) A series of large cards bearing the same figures in smooth paper for the enumeration of numbers above ten.

(r) Two boxes with small sticks for counting.

(s) The volume of drawings belonging specially to the method, and colored pencils.

(t) The frames for lacing, buttoning, etc., which are used for the education of the movements of the hand.

The Young Child's
Need for Structure

MANY investigators working with children, including Dr. Maria Montessori, have commented upon the need of the young child to order and master his environment by organizing in a meaningful way what is to him at first a chaos of sensory experience. Much of this ordering and mastering is achieved by the completion and repetition of relatively simple and discrete acts. However, the opportunity for individual practice is all too frequently unavailable in the homes from which many of our juvenile delinquents come. Because of the pressing shortage of space, the behavior of one individual is of necessity frequently interrupted or modified by the behavior of another. In fact, we can say that the juvenile delinquent, particularly one from a culturally deprived background, is often raised in a home where intense disruptive stimulation is the rule rather than the exception. In such a situation, the child does not have a chance to practice new behavior to the extent necessary for its mastery. Consequently he does not experience the sense of confidence and achievement that follows the mastering of an activity.

Interviews with delinquent children and extensive observation of their behavior suggest that these children have frequently resolved their need to order their immediate world by creating what to all outward appearances seems to be disorder and discord. However, upon closer examination, one finds that this apparent discord might well be their way of organizing their experience so that it is meaningful to them. It is quite possible, and, in the view of this writer, probable, that for many delinquents order consists of a kaleidoscopic sequence of events. This constantly shifting scene has come to represent "the expected" for the delinquent—the way things are now and will be.

Therefore, silence and orderliness may be unexpected, foreign experiences, leading to anxiety and discomfort. In a residential institution for delinquents we hear the blaring metallic dissonance of the music from their radios and record players which must, it seems, be played at full volume. Since such children are frequently from very crowded noisy homes where the parents habitually shout in order to be heard, they may respond only to a shouted command. However, in what to them is an oppressing pall of silence, they can sometimes be "shook up" by the deafening blast of a whisper. Such children will need considerable preparation before they can appreciate the Montessori "lesson of silence."

In recent years we have become increasingly and perhaps even acutely aware of the deleterious effects that cultural deprivation has on the development of the child. The environment of the child, especially in his early years, is now seen as exerting a pervasive and sometimes dramatic influence upon his mind and body. Lack of opportunity for learning to "order" his environment carries over into the deprived child's later development so that he is likely to remain retarded in relation to his fortunate contemporaries who learn to organize the world on a more conceptual basis.

Delinquents, whose expectations are based on an ever-changing world of rather intense stimuli, typically fail to adjust to schools geared to the traditional methods of teaching. These children are often extremely action-oriented and rather literalistic in their thinking. Because, unlike Montessori children, they have had the opportunity to master only a very small segment of their environment, they are still naturally concerned with things they can see, touch, manipulate, smell and, in general, experience through their senses.

Culturally deprived children and delinquents are simply not ready for the usual abstract educational fare. Small wonder that they are poor readers, hostile students, and ultimately dropouts. They have not had adequate opportunity to experience mastery over their environment at an early age. They have likewise had little opportunity to learn some techniques for controlling themselves. It is quite possible that this failure to achieve a considerable degree of self-mastery and mastery of their environment in their early years is reflected in later life as the feeling that they are victims of circumstances, incapable of self-direction and self-control.

Furthermore, their need to establish order as they know it brings about actions on their part which are in opposition to the larger order of the societal fabric. Their *order* involves delinquent behavior—the breaking of society's rules and regulations.

NEIL D. KOPPENHAVER, PH.D.

FREEDOM

If a new and scientific pedagogy is to arise from the *study of the individual,* such study must occupy itself with the observation of *free* children.

—*The Montessori Method,* p. 28

In The Montessori Method, *Dr. Montessori speaks of traditional education as "scholastic slavery." In* Pedagogical Anthropology, *she attacks the all-too-common "iron benches," poor lighting, and other oppressive features in the* schools of her day.[1] Here, Montessori sets forth the child's essential need for freedom. Expression of this freedom is possible in a prepared environment under the patient guardianship of an empathic adult whose forte is objective observation and study of individual children.

The didactic material, with the exercises of practical life, gymnastic exercises and other activities, provide an external "match" for the child's inner needs as a learner. But more important than a material or a method, of course, are the attitudes of the teacher, who must be psychologically secure enough to "diminish as the child expands." She must be "the patient one."

"Wait while observing," Montessori advises the educator. She uses the term "normalization" in her later books to refer to the process whereby the child allowed to work undisturbed for long periods of time in a prepared environment develops self-reliance and inner equilibrium. She is fond of referring to the child as a conquerer, and to his accomplishments as conquests. We read that china, glass, and knives are always included in the equipment of the Casa dei Bambini, and here she speaks of the "tureen of hot soup" that the children learn to handle confidently. Note again the value she attaches to order—order in the child's environment, movements, and mind; for the childhood years represent the sensitive period for establishing habits of order.

It was the achievement of Montessori, according to Nelly Wolffheim, to introduce what she has termed "self-occupation" into the nursery school. Wolffheim notes that the often hasty assistance of adults "may harm the child to an unpredictable extent." Thanks to Montessori, we have learned the disadvantages of "mistaken activity" by the teacher.[2]

Novelist Dorothy Canfield Fisher, who wrote A Montessori Mother after personal study of Montessori schools in Rome, noted the crucial importance of the auto-educative element in the Montessori method. According to Fisher, the central idea of the method, upon which everything rests, is "a full *recognition of the fact that no human being can be educated by anyone else." Each must do it himself, whether he is three or thirty.*[3]

Selected References

[1] Montessori, Maria, *Pedagogical Anthropology.* New York: Frederick Stokes, 1913.

[2] Wolffheim, Nelly, *Psychology in the Nursery School.* London: Gerald Duckworth and Co., Ltd., 1953.

[3] Fisher, Dorothy Canfield, *A Montessori Mother.* New York: Henry Holt, 1913.

Freedom

The success of these results is closely connected with the delicate intervention of the one who guides the children in their development. It is necessary for the teacher to *guide* the child without letting him feel her presence too much, so that she may be always ready to supply the desired help, but may never be the obstacle between the child and his experience.

A lesson in the ordinary use of the word cools the child's enthusiasm for the knowledge of things, just as it would cool the enthusiasm of adults. To keep alive that enthusiasm is the secret of real guidance, and it will not prove a difficult task, provided that the attitude toward the child's acts be that of respect, calm and waiting, and provided that he be left free in his movements and in his experiences.

Then we shall notice that the child has a personality which he is seeking to expand; he has initiative, he chooses his own work, persists in it, changes it according to his inner needs; he does not shirk effort; he rather goes in search of it, and with great joy overcomes obstacles within his capacity. He is sociable to the extent of wanting to share with every one his successes, his discoveries, and his little triumphs. There is therefore no need of intervention. "Wait while observing." That is the motto for the educator.

Let us wait, and be always ready to share in both the joys and the difficulties which the child experiences. He himself invites our sympathy, and we should respond fully and gladly. Let us have endless patience with his slow progress, and show enthusiasm and gladness at his successes. If we could say: "We are respectful and courteous in our dealings with children, we treat them as we should like to be treated ourselves," we should certainly have mastered a great educational principle and undoubtedly be setting an *example of good education*.

What we all desire for ourselves, namely, not to be disturbed in our work, not to find hindrances to our efforts, to have good friends ready to help us in times of need, to see them rejoice with us, to be on terms of equality with them, to be able to confide and trust in them—this is what we need for happy companionship. In the same way children are human beings to whom respect is due, superior to us by reason of their "innocence" and of the greater possibilities of their future. What we desire they desire also.

As a rule, however, we do not respect our children. We try to force them to follow us without regard to their special needs. We are overbearing with them, and above all, rude; and then we expect them to be submissive and well-behaved, knowing all the time how strong is their instinct of imitation and how touching their faith in and admiration of us. They will imitate us in any case. Let us treat them, therefore, with all the kindness which we would wish to help to develop in them. And by kindness is not meant caresses. Should we not call anyone who embraced us at the first time of meeting rude, vulgar and ill-bred? Kindness consists in interpreting the wishes of others, in conforming one's self to them, and sacrificing, if need be, one's own desire. This is the kindness which we must show towards children.

To find the interpretation of children's desires we must

study them scientifically, for their desires are often unconscious. They are the inner cry of life, which wishes to unfold according to mysterious laws. We know very little of the way in which it unfolds. Certainly the child is growing into a man by force of a divine action similar to that by which from nothing he became a child.

Our intervention in this marvelous process is *indirect*; we are here to offer to this life, which came into the world by itself, the *means* necessary for its development, and having done that we must await this development with respect.

Let us leave the life *free* to develop within the limits of the good, and let us observe this inner life developing. This is the whole of our mission. Perhaps as we watch we shall be reminded of the words of Him who was absolutely good, "Suffer the little children to come unto Me." That is to say, "Do not hinder them from coming, since, if they are left free and unhampered, they will come."

The child who has completed all the exercises above described, and is thus *prepared* for an advance toward unexpected conquests, is about four years old.

He is not an unknown quantity, as are children who have been left to gain varied and casual experiences by themselves, and who therefore differ in type and intellectual standard, not only according to their "natures," but especially according to the chances and opportunities they have found for their spontaneous inner formation.

Education has *determined an environment* for the children. Individual differences to be found in them can, therefore, be put down almost exclusively to each one's individual "nature." Owing to their environment which offers *means* adapted and measured to meet the needs of their psychical development, our children have acquired a fundamental type which is common to all. They have *coordinated* their movements in various kinds of manual work about the house, and so have acquired a characteristic independence of action, and initiative in the adaptation of their actions to their environment. Out of all this emerges a *personality*, for the children have become little men who are self-reliant.

The special attention necessary to handle small fragile objects without breaking them, and to move heavy articles without making a noise, has endowed the movements of the whole body with a lightness and grace which are characteristic of our children. It is a deep feeling of responsibility which has brought them to such a pitch of perfection. For instance, when they carry three or four tumblers at a time, or a tureen of hot soup, they know that they are responsible not only for the objects, but also for the success of the meal which at that moment they are directing. In the same way each child feels the responsibility of the "silence," of the prevention of harsh sounds, and he knows how to cooperate for the general good in keeping the environment, not only orderly, but quiet and calm. Indeed, our children have taken the road which leads them to mastery of themselves.

But their formation is due to a deeper psychological work still, arising from the education of the senses. In addition to ordering their environment and ordering themselves in their outward personalities, they have also ordered the inner world of their minds.

The didactic material, in fact, does not offer to the child the "content" of the mind, but the *order* for that "content." It causes him to distinguish identities from differences, extreme differences from fine gradations, and to classify, under conceptions of quality and of quantity, the most varying sensations appertaining to surfaces, colors, dimensions, forms and sounds. The mind has formed itself by a special exercise of attention, observing, comparing, and classifying.

The mental attitude acquired by such an exercise leads the child to make ordered observations in his environment, observations which prove as interesting to him as discoveries, and so stimulate him to multiply them indefinitely and to form in his mind a rich "content" of clear ideas.

II

THE IMPORTANCE OF MOVEMENT IN EDUCATION

These children, occupied in dressing, cleaning, washing, combing, cleansing, and arranging their environment, work themselves. As a result, they love useful objects so much that they will preserve a piece of paper for years, and instead of knocking against furniture, and breaking objects, they perfect their movements.

—*Spontaneous Activity in Education*, p. 302

Learning Through Movement

MONTESSORI says in her *Advanced Montessori Method* that "it is action which counts." Elsewhere in the same book she explains that "the child must move about a great deal, to coordinate his movements, which are not yet under control." Her "motor education" is designed to accomplish at least three purposes: 1) to aid the normal development of movements involved in walking, breathing, speech, etc.; 2) to foster this development when the child shows himself backward or abnormal in any way; and 3) to encourage those movements which are useful in the everyday acts of life such as dressing, undressing, carrying objects, etc.

In the accounts of human learning during infancy and early childhood written by Maria Montessori, Jean Piaget, Arnold Gesell, Edith Cobb, Lois Barclay Murphy, Gordon Allport and other researchers, the acquisition of motor skills is seen as a crucial ingredient in the young child's understanding of and adjustment to the world of persons, things and ideas.

While the exact physiological mechanisms operative in perception and cognition are still only little understood, the inherent motility of the human organism and the behavioral changes that accrue from sensorimotor activity offer observable and predictable evidence of the basic role of movement in learning.

The first feeble "whole body" responses of the newborn, the all-important tonic neck reflex, the strong hand grasp of the baby, the various crawling and creeping movements leading to walking, the pincer grasp of oppositional thumb

59

and index finger—all these and many more are indicators of ever-more complex patterns of action to come. All are part and parcel of the ontogenetic "blueprint" of human growth and development. They represent the structural and functional units for growing and knowing, being and behaving.

Just as structure and function are interdependent, so are the motor and sensory components of learning. By actively exploring, manipulating, playing with, contemplating, and enjoying the things, people and ideas of his world, the young child learns to see, hear, touch and know this world, to assign meanings based on his personal experience and dependent in large measure upon movement.

The young child's movements are his first learnings, his first attempts to organize his own world on his own terms. With the maturation of his "distance" senses (sight and hearing) his motor interactions are extended and refined. The world of "arm's length" becomes a world "beyond arm's length," the world of "me" becomes a world of "beyond me." The development of general movement patterns yields to the development of specific movement patterns, with unstructured movements becoming coordinated and random movements becoming purposeful and efficient.

Dr. G. N. Getman, in summarizing the researches of the developmental psychologists, notes that "a child does not move to move, but to act." He reports a direct relationship between how well a child moves about in his world in organizing his actions (and utilizing his energy) into total behavior patterns, and how well he interprets his world through his visual mechanisms. Vision (the integrate of all the sensory modes) is seen as the catalyst between activity and comprehension. In these terms, eyes steer or guide the early general movements in exploring the world. In manipulating the things in his world, eyes and hands work in combination. As experience is elaborated and skills are practiced, vision provides sufficient information without the movements previously necessary. With the development of language for communication with others, speech eventually replaces the need for direct action. Visualization patterns of past actions or similar experiences come eventually to substitute for action, speech, and time. Getman's observations support the findings of Gesell, Halstead, Hunt, Bruner and others in perceptual-motor aspects of cognition and conceptualization.

Renewed interest in the Montessori Method, the cognitive enrichment preschool programs in slum areas, interdisciplinary researches on psychophysiological processes, and the revival of tactual and kinesthetic teaching materials all reflect a reawakened awareness of the experiences of the preschool years as crucial in later intellectual development. We have, as educators, yet to pledge full allegiance to the role of motor mimicry and skills acquisition in the processes of understanding, coping with and adjusting to the world. If, indeed, learning is predicated on movement . . . if interaction with the environment is essential for gathering information and storing it in experiential units for future reference . . . if out of movement patterns comes a system of "perceptual-match" relationships prerequisite to concept formation . . . if spatial, form, and time concepts are nurtured in the direct bodily movements through space and time in patterned directions in early life experiences . . . then reevaluation of pedagogical practices is long overdue, and the translation of known psychophysiological principles to action programs is crucial in an increasingly complex world.

In her *Handbook,* Montessori has given us the outline for a comprehensive program of motor, sensory, and intellectual education which could well serve as a guide for those concerned with all aspects of development of preschool and elementary school children.

GERTRUDE R. JUSTISON, ED.D.

Selected References

[1] Allport, Gordon W., *Pattern and Growth in Personality*. New York: Holt, Rinehart and Winston, 1961.

[2] Gesell, Arnold, *et al.*, *Vision: Its Development in Infant and Child*. New York: Haeber, 1949.

[3] Getman, G. N., and Elmer R. Kane, *The Physiology of Readiness*. Minneapolis, Minnesota: P.A.S.S., Inc., P.O. Box 1004, 1964.

[4] Murphy, Lois B., *The Widening World of Childhood*. New York: Basic Books, Inc., 1954.

[5] Piaget, Jean, *The Construction of Reality in the Child*. New York: Basic Books, Inc., 1954.

MOTOR EDUCATION

True rest for muscles, intended by nature for action,
is in orderly action.

—*The Montessori Method*, p. 354

MONTESSORI, *never one to confuse forced immobility of children with virtue, created a learning environment basically different from the traditional classroom format. Montessori children are free to move as they learn, for she considers freedom and work essential to the normal child's self-development (and just as essential for the improvement of children who have suffered trauma in a harsh environment).*

Visitors to a Montessori school are sometimes surprised to find no teacher's desk, and to see most of the children working on the floor; but Montessori, discerning the intimate relationship between movement and mental development, recognized that the child must be provided with the opportunity to move as he learns. This movement should not be of a random nature, but should be directed toward useful activity, and "in the service of learning." The teacher, to be effective, must often work with the children on their level, upon the carpet, rather than lecture to them from the front of the room. The young child's body, as well as his mind, is "absorbent," and the motor skills and coordination achieved will be greatly influenced by the various opportunities in his environment for motor training and practice.

The directress may be said to help give direction to the child's movement, more often by example than by word, recognizing that coordinated movement is more efficient and less tiring than its opposite. When explaining an action, her own motions must be slow enough for the child to follow, and often repeated. She must adjust her adult rhythm to that of the child. Much motor learning is imitative, hence the need for exemplary behavior by the directress, who demonstrates carefully and patiently.

Montessori says the teacher should "count her words," that is, utilize carefully chosen words purposefully. Her emphasis should be upon showing rather than telling, employing both exemplary gesture and speech. When an activity is being presented to a child for the first time, he should be watching the teacher's hands, not her mouth, as she carefully does the exercise. After the child is invited to do the exercise, the teacher does not intrude with all manner of verbal clues. Perhaps, those writers who have discussed the "short" attention span of preschoolers have really been talking about the inability of young children to follow long verbal explanations.

In the motor area, as in the sensory and "intellectual" areas, the directress, with her students, analyzes the skills to be acquired, breaking these skills into sub-tasks which are mastered in turn, leading to their orchestration in graceful activity. The exercises of practical life provide the miniature society of the Montessori classroom with group endeavors such as caring for the environment, and preparing and serving a meal, enabling children to learn how to move and work together harmoniously.

The Biography of a Baby, *Millicent Shinn's classic description of the sensory, motor and language development* of a baby during its first year, details the child's basic need to explore its environment. She speaks of the baby's "great and active interest in studying the visible world." By the end of the fourth month the baby had learned the appearance of many things, and was well aware when its world was "in any way changed." She notes that "it is an epoch of tremendous importance when the baby first, with real attention, brings sight and touch and muscle feeling to bear together on an object." Clothes cause babies to "lose a great deal of their normal activity," so a chance to roll about nude in a warm room is a "great thing for a baby." By nine months the infant was indeed a true explorer.[1]

Bela Mittelmann believes there is a human motility, or motor urge, present throughout life but dominant at the beginning of the second year and remaining dominant for several years.[2] Erik Erikson refers to the young child's "sense of industry" and to his "pleasure of work completion." The "playing" child is actually advancing toward new stages of "real mastery." It is the playing adult, he says, who is involved in "an artificial reality."[3]

Margaret Ribble reminds us that for too long we have neglected the infant's growth and development. Artificial schedules have been allowed to obstruct the spontaneous natural behavior of the healthy baby. She notes that sudden changes "exert an extremely disorganizing influence on nervous integration."[4] Werner Wolff emphasizes that the adult should appreciate the basic difference between the adult mind and that of the child. Wolff believes that the child's rhythmic organization is a vital indicator of intelligence itself.[5]

Selected References

[1] Shinn, Millicent, *The Biography of a Baby*. Boston: Houghton Mifflin, 1900.

[2] Mittelmann, Bela, "Motility in Infants, Children and Adults." *The Psychoanalytic Study of the Child*, Vol. 9. New York: International Universities Press, 1954. Pp. 142-147.

[3] Erickson, Erik, "Identity and the Life Cycle." Selected papers in *Psychological Issues*. Vol. I, No. 1, 1959, Monograph 1, New York International Universities Press. See especially pp. 52, 57, 71, 85-86, 100.

[4] Ribble, Margaret, *The Rights of Infants: Early Psychological Needs and Their Satisfaction*. New York: Columbia University Press, Seventh Printing, December, 1946.

[5] Wolff, Werner, *The Personality of the Preschool Child*. New York: Greene and Stratton, 1947. See Chapter 8, "Intelligence in the Preschool Child."

Motor Education

The education of the movements is very complex, as it must correspond to all the coordinated movements which the child has to establish in his physiological organism. The child, if left without guidance, is disorderly in his movements, and these disorderly movements are the *special characteristic of the little child*. In fact, he "never keeps still," and "touches everything." This is what forms the child's so-called "unruliness" and "naughtiness."

The adult would deal with him by checking these movements, with the monotonous and useless repetition "keep still." As a matter of fact, in these movements the little one is seeking the very exercise which will organize and coordinate the movements useful to man. We must, therefore, desist from the useless attempt to reduce the child to a state of immobility. We should rather give "order" to his movements, leading them to those actions toward which his efforts are actually tending. This is the aim of muscular education at this age. Once a direction is given to them, the child's movements are made toward a definite end, so that he himself grows quiet and contented, and becomes an active worker, a being calm and full of joy. This education of the movements is one of the principal factors in producing that outward appearance of "discipline" to be found in the "Children's Houses." I have already spoken at length on this subject in my other books.

Muscular education has reference to:

The primary movements of everyday life (walking, rising, sitting, handling objects).

The care of the person.

Management of the household.

Gardening.

Manual work.

Gymnastic exercises.

Rhythmic movements.

In the care of the person the first step is that of dressing and undressing. For this end there is in my didactic material a collection of frames to which are attached pieces of material, leather, etc. These can be buttoned, hooked, tied together—in fact, joined in all the different ways which our civilization has invented for fastening our clothing, shoes, etc. The teacher, sitting by the child's side, performs the necessary movements of the fingers very slowly and deliberately, separating the movements themselves into their different parts, and letting them be seen clearly and minutely.

For example, one of the first actions will be the adjustment of the two pieces of material in such a way that the edges to be fastened together touch one another from top to bottom. Then, if it is a buttoning frame, the teacher will show the child the different stages of the action. She will take hold of the button, set it opposite the buttonhole, make it enter the buttonhole completely, and adjust it carefully in its place above. In the same way, to teach a child to tie a bow, she will separate the stage in which he ties the ribbons together from that in which he makes the bows.

In the film of a "Children's House" there is a picture which shows an entire lesson in the tying of the bows with the ribbons. These lessons are not necessary for all the children, as they learn from one another, and of their own accord come with great patience to analyze the movements, performing them separately very slowly and carefully. The child can sit in a comfortable position and hold his frame on the table. As he fastens and unfastens the same frame many times over with great interest, he acquires an unusual deftness of hand, and becomes possessed with the desire to fasten real clothes whenever he has the opportunity. We see the smallest children *wanting* to dress themselves and their companions. They go in search of amusement of this kind, and defend themselves with all their might against the adult who would try to help them.

In the same way for the teaching of the other and larger movements, such as washing, setting the table, etc., the directress must at the beginning intervene; teaching the child with few or no words at all, but with very precise actions. She teaches all the movements: how to sit, to rise from one's seat, to take up and lay down objects, and to offer them gracefully to others. In the same way she teaches the children to set the plates one upon the other and lay them on the table without making any noise.

The children learn easily and show an interest and surprising care in the performance of these actions. In classes where there are many children it is necessary to arrange for the children to take turns in the various household duties, such as housework, serving at table, and washing dishes. The children readily respect such a system of turns. There is no need to ask them to do this work, for they come spontaneously—even little ones of two and a half years old—to offer to do their share, and it is frequently most touching to watch their efforts to imitate, to remember, and, finally, to conquer their difficulty. Professor Jacoby, of New York, was once much moved as he watched a child, who was little more than two years old and not at all intelligent in appearance, standing perplexed because he could not remember whether the fork should be set at the right hand or the left. He remained a long while meditating and evidently using all the powers of his mind. The other children older than he watched him with admiration, marveling, like ourselves, at the life developing under our eyes.

The instructions of the teacher consist then merely in a hint, a touch—enough to give a start to the child. The rest develops of itself. The children learn from one another and throw themselves into the work with enthusiasm and delight. This atmosphere of quiet activity develops a fellow feeling, an attitude of mutual aid, and, most wonderful of all, an intelligent interest on the part of the older children in the progress of their little companions. It is enough just to set a child in these peaceful surroundings for him to feel perfectly at home. In the film referred to earlier, the actual work in a "Children's House" may be seen. The children are moving about, each one fulfilling his own task, whilst the teacher is in a corner watching. Pictures were taken also of the children engaged in the care of the house, that is, in the care both of their persons and of their surroundings. They can be seen washing their faces, polishing their shoes, washing the furniture, polishing the metal indicators of the pedometer, brushing the carpets, etc. In the work of laying the table the children are seen quite by themselves, dividing the work among themselves, carrying the plates, spoons, knives and forks, etc., and, finally, sitting down at the tables where the little waitresses serve the hot soup.

Again, gardening and manual work are a great pleasure to our children. Gardening is already well known as a feature of infant education, and it is recognized by all that plants and animals attract the children's care and attention. The ideal of the "Children's Houses" in this respect is to imitate the best in the present usage of those schools which owe their inspiration more or less to Mrs. Latter.

For manual instruction we have chosen clay work, consisting of the construction of little tiles, vases and bricks.

These may be made with the help of simple instruments, such as molds. The completion of the work should be the aim always kept in view, and, finally, all the little objects made by the children should be glazed and baked in the furnace. The children themselves learn to line a wall with shining white or colored tiles wrought in various designs, or, with the help of mortar and a trowel, to cover the floor with little bricks. They also dig out foundations and then use their bricks to build division walls, or entire little houses for the chickens.

Among the gymnastic exercises that which must be considered the most important is that of the "line." A line is described in chalk or paint upon a large space of floor. Instead of one line, there may also be two concentric lines, elliptical in form. The children are taught to walk upon these lines like tightrope walkers, placing their feet one in front of the other. To keep their balance they make efforts exactly similar to those of real tightrope walkers, except that they have no danger with which to reckon, as the lines are only *drawn* upon the floor. The teacher herself performs the exercise, showing clearly how she sets her feet, and the children imitate her without any necessity for her to speak. At first it is only certain children who follow her, and when she has shown them how to do it, she withdraws, leaving the phenomenon to develop of itself.

The children for the most part continue to walk, adapting their feet with great care to the movement they have seen, and making efforts to keep their balance so as not to fall. Gradually the other children draw near and watch and also make an attempt. Very little time elapses before the whole of the two ellipses or the one line is covered with children balancing themselves, and continuing to walk around, watching their feet with an expression of deep attention on their faces.

Music may then be used. It should be a very simple

march, the rhythm of which is not obvious at first, but which accompanies and enlivens the spontaneous efforts of the children.

When they have learned in this way to master their balance the children have brought the act of walking to a remarkable standard of perfection, and have acquired, in addition to security and composure in their natural gait, an unusually graceful carriage of the body. The exercise on the line can afterward be made more complicated in various ways. The first application is that of calling forth rhythmic exercise by the sound of a march upon the piano. When the same march is repeated during several days, the children end by feeling the rhythm and by following it with movements of their arms and feet. They also accompany the exercises on the line with songs.

Little by little the music is *understood* by the children. They finish, as in Miss George's school at Washington, by singing over their daily work with the didactic material. The "Children's House" then resembles a hive of bees humming as they work.

As to the little gymnasium, of which I speak in my book *The Montessori Method,* one piece of apparatus is particularly practical. This is the "fence," from which the children hang by their arms, freeing their legs from the heavy weight of the body and strengthening the arms. This fence has also the advantage of being useful in a garden for the purpose of dividing one part from another, as, for example, the flower beds from the garden walks, and it does not detract in any way from the appearance of the garden.

Prescribing A
"Prepared Environment"

MONTESSORI has noted that all illness may involve a psychological coefficient, for "psychological life and physical life are closely connected." She says that a "bad child" should as a general rule be taken to see a physician "because it is almost certain that he is a sick child." Referring to her schools as "houses of health," she observes that many illnesses may disappear when children are allowed to function in a "prepared environment."

We know that anxiety and stress may cause some skin conditions and aggravate others; hostility and rage can be important elements in the etiology of peptic ulcer and colitis. Unresolved dependency upon the mother is a possible factor in the precipitation of asthma. These and other illnesses which may be influenced by the emotions manifest themselves in all age groups; peptic ulcers have been found in an occasional three-year-old. Often, exacerbations of chronic diseases such as rheumatoid arthritis are triggered by emotional stress which the patient has not learned to handle. Many experimental studies have shown a definite relationship between one's state of mind and one's susceptibility to disease.

Montessori tells us that "man is a unity," whose sensitive mind-body balance necessitates the physician's concern with the prevention of mental as well as physical disorders. The roots of both often may be traced back to the preschool years; and emotional stress in the adult frequently causes him to regress to childhood patterns of adjustment. Because the growing individual is more amenable to modification of his responses than the biologically mature person, the physician who treats the child has a unique opportunity to promote ultimately the mental as well as the physical health of the community. He must recognize any symptoms of undue tension operating within the child, and then help the parents to develop more adequate methods of child rearing.

An invaluable aid in this phase of his work may be found in Dr. Maria Montessori's concept of the "prepared environment." This environment contains the necessities for a sound psychological climate, and engenders forces important to the maturation of the child. For example, the Montessori "ground rules," if properly enforced, ensure that the child learns that he is a person of value, yet they also teach him to recognize the value of his associates and to respect them. They give him the freedom to engage in the work of his choice without interruption; they also ensure that he does not deprive another child of this freedom. The materials which are self-correcting allow him to engage in meaningful tasks and to experience and evaluate for himself the worth of his own accomplishments.

The physician who is well versed in the purposes of the ground rules, in the nature of the sensitive periods of the child's growth and development, and in the logic of the order and timing of the presentation of the Montessori materials, can help the parents adapt many of the features of the "prepared environment" to the home. Most parents want to be good parents and are willing to consider a course of action suggested by the child's physician. The parents can be helped to understand the importance of the child's need to achieve self-discipline and independence. If the parents can be given some concrete methods to help promote the child's self-direction, they may be able to modify any tendencies, for example, to overprotect their youngsters. Thus, the child will be allowed to assume responsibility commensurate with his age; he will know work with the hands and work with the mind; he will recognize responsibility and work as realities of life and will be able to face them later without anxiety, insecurity and regression. Likewise, the parent who has high expectations for the child may be helped to understand the child's limitations and will learn not to arouse unnecessary rage, hostility and frustrations by unreasonable demands and criticisms.

Perhaps the philosophy and principles underlying the Montessori "prepared environment" may ultimately attain more importance as guidelines for the furtherance of general mental and physical health than as mere pedagogical formulas. Although the educational achievements of Montessori children can be remarkable, the emphasis is really not on how much the child can achieve quickly, but, rather, is on giving the child an opportunity to gain mastery at his own speed in all areas pertaining to living. The "auto-educative" approach enables him to achieve his own potential, and to develop independence and a sense of security that will allow him to establish order and peace in his own personal life.

ELIZABETH J. OLIVEIRA, M.D.

THE MONTESSORI PEDOMETER

The use of the weighing machine, both at home and in school cannot be too strongly recommended.

—*Pedagogical Anthropology*, p. 177

The pedometer is an ingenious device for taking certain physical measurements of the child. It is a practical example of Montessori's characteristic merging of the pedagogical with the biological, reflecting her own medical background and her concern for systematic measuring and recording of various aspects of the child's development.

The Montessori Pedometer

My pedometer forms part of the equipment of a "Children's House." After various modifications I have now reduced this instrument to a very practical form.

The purpose of the pedometer, as its name shows, is to measure the children. It consists of a wide rectangular board, forming the base, from the center of which rise two wooden posts held together at the top by a narrow flat piece of metal. To each post is connected a horizontal metal rod—the indicator—which runs up and down by means of a casing, also of metal. This metal casing is made in one piece with the indicator, to the end of which is fixed an india-rubber ball. On one side, that is to say, behind one of the two tall vertical wooden posts, there is a small seat, also of wood. The two tall wooden posts are graduated. The post to which the seat is fixed is graduated from the surface of the seat to the top, while the other is graduated from the wooden board at the base to the top, *i.e.* to a height of 1.5 meters. On the side containing the seat the height of the child seated is measured, on the other side the child's full stature. The practical value of this instrument lies in the possibility of measuring two children at the same time, and in the fact that the children themselves cooperate in taking the measurements. In fact, they learn to take off their shoes and to place themselves in the correct position on the pedometer. They find no difficulty in raising and lowering the metal indicators, which are held so firmly in place by means of the metal casing that they cannot deviate from their horizontal position even when used by inexpert hands. Moreover they run extremely easily, so that very little strength is required to move them. The little india-rubber balls prevent the children from hurting themselves should they inadvertently knock their heads against the metal indicator.

The children are very fond of the pedometer. "Shall we measure ourselves?" is one of the proposals which they make most willingly and with the greatest likelihood of finding many of their companions to join them. They also take great care of the pedometer, dusting it, and polishing its metal parts. All the surfaces of the pedometer are so smooth and well polished that they invite the care that is taken of them, and by their appearance when finished fully repay the trouble taken.

The pedometer represents the scientific part of the method, because it has reference to the anthropological and psychological study made of the children, each of whom has his own biographical record. This biographical record follows the history of the child's development according to the observations which it is possible to make by the application of my method. This subject is dealt with at length in my other books. A series of films has been taken of the pedometer at a moment when the children are being measured. They are seen coming of their own accord, even the very smallest, to take their places at the instrument.

SENSORY EDUCATION AND MUSIC

From simple didactic objects which primarily attract the senses, the children pass to objects which teach reading and writing, and later grammar, arithmetic, geometry, drawing, music, etc.

—*The Organization of Intellectual Work in School*, p. 718

The Child as Observer

MONTESSORI, who speaks of "the pedagogical method of observation," says that "the education of the senses makes men observers." Such education has as its aim "the refinement of the differential perception of stimuli by means of repeated exercises."[1] The degree of success of the teacher will be largely determined by her ability as an observer. Montessori recognizes this clearly. "Here lies the essential point: from her scientific preparation, the teacher must bring not only the capacity, but the desire, to observe natural phenomena."[2] The Montessori Method, then, both for the pupil and the teacher is, in a word, *observation*.

From the Optometric Extension Program Foundation have come research, methods and a dynamic theory of vision enabling optometrists to move beyond outmoded traditional concepts of looking at children's visual problems from adult standards based on optical defects. In the field of child vision care, optometry is applying the new and dynamic concepts coming from advances in child development, psychology, and education. No longer can we equate the development of human vision with the physics of an eyeball. The belief that 20/20 acuity constitutes all there is to seeing cannot support modern educational psychology, which demands seeing for comprehension, seeing for problem solving, and seeing to formulate language and to encourage better communication in human relations. Dr. G. N. Getman and his associates in the Foundation's section on Optometric Child Vision Care and Guidance are calling for a team approach by optometrists, psychologists, and educators in caring for the educational problems of children.

Optometry guides children in the developmental processes of *learning to see*; education guides children in the academic processes that utilize *seeing to learn*; child psychology appraises the efforts of those who assist children in the processes of *learning to learn*. Care and guidance based upon developmental principles are assisting many children to reach more adequate achievement levels in a culture that places primary emphasis on the accurate visual interpretation of a printed page. It must also be recognized, however, that a child's first teachers are his parents.

In developing clinical programs to foster this team approach among parents, optometrists, educators, and psychologists, a mutual understanding of the visual development of the child is basic. Through the leadership of Dr. A. M. Skeffington, Educational Director of the Optometric Extension Program, a significant portion of the optometric profession has become more clinically interested in the *function of vision* than in the *defects of eyes*. From this pragmatic approach to vision as a learned developmental process, the following conclusions have been reached and published by the Child Care Section:[3]

READINESS IS A PRODUCT OF EXPERIENCE

A child's readiness to take advantage of new learning opportunities depends upon how adequately he has understood, organized, and utilized his preschool experiences.

EXPERIENCE DEPENDS UPON MOVEMENT

The adequacy of preschool learning experiences is directly related to how well the child has learned to move in organized patterns of action throughout his own expanding world from birth to the day he enters the classroom.

MOVEMENT IS ESSENTIAL FOR VISUAL DEVELOPMENT

There is a direct relationship between how well a child moves about in his world in organizing his actions into total behavior patterns, and how well he interprets his world through the use of his visual mechanisms.

VISION IS DEVELOPED

The child's ability visually to interpret the world and his place in it is learned; therefore, visual perception is learned. It is properly learned only to the extent of a child's action and interaction with *his* world. These actions and interactions by the child are not always spontaneous, and must be encouraged and/or arranged by adults; thus, ultimate visual abilities are learned by the child.

DEVELOPED ABILITIES CAN BE IMPROVED

Because visual abilities are learned, the optometrist must provide proper vision care assuring the child the ocular and visual perceptual skills needed for participation in the classroom program. The optometrist should provide parents with enough clinical information to direct the visual guidance program of their child. Consultations with teacher and psychologist concerning visual-perception problems that may be hindering the child's academic progress can further enhance the total guidance program.

The reader will discern in Montessori's *Handbook* many elements of her method consonant with the above conclusions. These elements include recognition of the importance of preschool experience; primacy of motor education; emphasis upon multisensory learning; perception as a learned process; use of the interdisciplinary "team" approach to childhood education; and the essential role of parents as team members.

PAUL LEWIS, O.D.

Selected References

[1] Montessori, Maria, *The Montessori Method.* New York: Frederick Stokes, 1912. P. 86.

[2] *Ibid.,* p. 87.

[3] *A Brighter Way of Life for All Children.* Duncan, Oklahoma: Child Care Section, Optometric Extension Program Foundation. *Note:* Certain material from this booklet has been reproduced with the permission of Dr. G. N. Getman, Chairman of the Child Care Section.

SENSORY EDUCATION

Our sensory material, in fact, analyzes and represents the attributes of things: dimensions, forms, colors, smoothness or roughness of surface, weight, temperature, flavor, noise, sounds. It is the qualities of the objects, not the objects themselves, which are important.

—*Spontaneous Activity in Education*, p. 203

The brilliant learning theorist Professor B. F. Skinner is sometimes referred to as the "father" of the modern teaching machine. In view of her experiments in developing a "programmed" approach to perceptual training, it is perhaps not inappropriate to identify Dr. Maria Montessori as the "great-grandmother" of such devices.

In this section, the reader will be able to see clearly the thorough study that Montessori invested in the development of a sequential didactic material. Note how the material, or apparatus, progresses from the concrete to the abstract, from the simple to the complex, as the child's tasks of discrimination become ever more challenging.

Montessori emphasized the importance of repetition in learning; and she was aware that the child, at certain stages in the learning process, displays a love of repetition, of repeated action. Because much of the child's learning is imitative, he should be exposed to desirable models as he acquires patterns of speech, movement, etc. These exemplary models are especially important during the child's sensitive period for language development and muscular activity.

Note that the role of the Montessori teacher, as she demonstrates the sensory and motor exercises, for example, is far from passive. However, after an individual lesson the child is in direct contact with the materials himself, free to proceed at his own rate as the instrument of his own learning, much of which is tactile-oriented. Sensory education lays the foundation for language development which embraces listening, speaking, writing, and reading.

Montessori's concept of "the child as teacher" has at least three aspects. The child teaches other children, sometimes directly, often indirectly. The child, in a pedagogy of "auto-education," teaches himself. Finally, the child teaches adults. For example, the "teacher as experimenter" implies continual learning on the teacher's part as she observes the child's reactions. Such phrases as "his face meanwhile expressing his pleasure and interest" indicate that the teacher herself is a "student of visage." The reader will note that Montessori is fond of illustrating a point by referring to an observation of her own or one of her teachers.

Physiologist W. Grey Walter, who has pioneered the study of human brain wave patterns (electroencephalography), has observed that "Dr. Montessori initiated her revolution in free discipline and sensory training by raising the attainment of mental defectives to the level of the State examinations in Italy. . . ."[1]

There is much in his seminal text, The Living Brain, to support Montessori. He describes the sense of touch as "the most vital of the senses,"[2] and says that "association comes early and easy to the human baby," with repetition of any kind tracing "each time more plainly a pattern in the brain."[3] In her Method, Montessori says that "it is exactly in the repetition of the exercises that the education of the senses consists."

Walter's observation that "practice makes perfect in a great diversity of circumstances"[4] reminds one of Montessori's belief that "what strengthens any developing power is practice, and practice is still needed after the basic power has been obtained" (The Absorbent Mind). Walter's statement that "what the nervous system receives from the sense organs is information about differences—about ratios between stimuli"[5] can be related to Montessori's use of the term "mathematical mind," which refers to the young child's *mathematical bent, his predisposition to precision, order, detail, and quantification.*

In The Organization of Behavior, *Donald Hebb describes a provocative neurological theory of learning in which early experience plays a crucial role in structuring perception. According to Hebb, repeated stimulation of receptors leads to the organization of functional units which he terms "cell assemblies." With further experience the "cell assemblies" combine to form "phase sequences." He considers all learning as utilizing and building on earlier learning, and notes the tendency of much early learning to be permanent.[6] Inasmuch as a stimulating environment is completely necessary as a determinant of intellectual growth,[7] childhood experience will greatly influence the level of adult problem solving.[8] In a deprived environment, the nervous system may fail to learn the forms necessary for the individual's mastery of our increasingly complex world.*

Charles Eliot, for forty years president of Harvard, noted that education has neglected the training of sight, hearing, smell, taste, and touch "to a most extraordinary degree." He considered quickness and accuracy in all the senses to be of "high value to the individual throughout life," with some slight but unusual superiority in one or more of the senses often becoming "the real basis of success in life."[9] Like Montessori, Eliot felt that a principal goal of education should be the awakening and training of the power of concentrated attention, the skillful teacher being one who is able to discover the means of interesting the child enough in a mental activity to concentrate his attention.[10]

According to Eliot, it was Ralph Waldo Emerson, "the greatest of American philosophers," who "first in this country declared that the possession of some manual skill, some power to do work with his body, with his eyes, his ears, his hands, was essential to the right quality of the cultivated man."[11] Emerson, speaking of the child in his essay Education, *says:*

He has a secret; wonderful methods in him; he is—every child—a new style of man; give him time and opportunity. Talk of Columbus and Newton! I tell you the child just born in yonder hovel is the beginning of a revolution as great as theirs. But you must have the believing and prophetic eye. Have the self-command you wish to inspire. Your teaching and discipline must have the reserve and taciturnity of Nature. Teach them to hold their tongues by holding your own. Say little; do not snarl; do not chide; but govern by the eye. See what they need, and that the right thing is done.

For Emerson, "the secret of Education lies in respecting the pupil." The works of Emerson were known to Montessori, who refers to them in her own writings, such as The Secret of Childhood.[12]

Selected References

[1] Walter, W. Grey, *The Living Brain.* New York: W. W. Norton, 1953. P. 269.

[2] Ibid., p. 75.

[3] Ibid., p. 142.

[4] Ibid., p. 138.

[5] Ibid., p. 135.

[6] Hebb, Donald O., *The Organization of Behavior.* New York: John Wiley, 1949. P. 109.

[7] Ibid., p. 302.

[8] Ibid., p. 120.

[9] Eliot, Charles, *Education for Efficiency.* Boston: Houghton Mifflin, 1909. P. 6.

[10] Ibid., p. 13.

[11] Eliot, Charles W., *The Tendency to the Concrete and Practical in Modern Education.* Boston: Houghton Mifflin, 1913. P. 10.

[12] Montessori, Maria, *The Secret of Childhood.* London: Longmans, Green and Co., 1936.

Sensory Education

My didactic material offers to the child the *means* for what may be called "sensory education."

In the box of material the first three objects which are

likely to attract the attention of a little child from two and a half to three years old are three solid pieces of wood, in each of which is inserted a row of ten small cylinders, or sometimes discs, all furnished with a button for a handle. In the first case there is a row of cylinders of the same height, but with a diameter which decreases from thick to thin. In the second there are cylinders which decrease in all dimensions, and so are either larger or smaller, but always of the same shape.

Lastly, in the third case, the cylinders have the same diameter but vary in height, so that, as the size decreases, the cylinder gradually becomes a little disc in form.

The first cylinders vary in two dimensions (the section); the second in all three dimensions; the third in one dimension (height). The order which I have given refers to the degree of *ease* with which the child performs the exercises.

The exercise consists in taking out the cylinders, mixing them and putting them back in the right place. It is performed by the child as he sits in a comfortable position at a little table. He exercises his hands in the delicate act of taking hold of the button with the tips of one or two fingers, and in the little movements of the hand and arm as he mixes the cylinders, *without letting them fall* and *without making too much noise,* and puts them back again each in its own place.

In these exercises the teacher may, in the first instance, intervene, merely taking out the cylinders, mixing them carefully on the table and then showing the child that he is to put them back, but without performing the action herself. Such intervention, however, is almost always found to be unnecessary, for the children *see* their companions at work, and thus are encouraged to imitate them.

They like to do it *alone*; in fact, sometimes almost in private for fear of inopportune help.

But how is the child to find the right place for each of the little cylinders which lie mixed upon the table? He first makes trials; it often happens that he places a cylinder which is too large for the empty hole over which he puts it. Then, changing its place, he tries others until the cylinder goes in. Again, the contrary may happen; that is to say, the cylinder may slip too easily into a hole too big for it. In that case it has taken a place which does not belong to it at all, but to a larger cylinder. In this way one cylinder at the end will be left out without a place, and it will not be possible to find one that fits. Here the child cannot help seeing his mistake in concrete form. He is perplexed, his little mind is faced with a problem which interests him intensely. Before, all the cylinders fitted, now there is one that will not fit. The little one stops, frowning, deep in thought. He begins to feel the little buttons and finds that some cylinders have too much room. He thinks that perhaps they are out of their right place and tries to place them correctly. He repeats the process again and again, and finally he succeeds. Then it is that he breaks into a smile of triumph. The exercise arouses the intelligence of the child; he wants to repeat it right from the beginning and, having learned by experience, he makes another attempt. Little children from three to three and a half years old have repeated the exercise up to *forty* times without losing their interest in it.

If the second set of cylinders and then the third are presented, the *change* of shape strikes the child and reawakens his interest.

The material which I have described serves to *educate the eye* to distinguish *difference in dimension,* for the child ends by being able to recognize at a glance the larger or the smaller hole which exactly fits the cylinder which he holds in his hand. The educative process is based on this: that the control of the error lies in *the material itself,* and the child has concrete evidence of it.

The desire of the child to attain an end which he knows,

leads him to correct himself. It is not a teacher who makes him notice his mistake and shows him how to correct it, but it is a complex work of the child's own intelligence which leads to such a result.

Hence at this point there begins the process of auto-education.

The aim is not an external one; that is to say, it is *not* the object that the child should learn how to place the cylinders, and *that he should know how to perform an exercise.*

The aim is an inner one, namely, that the child train himself to observe; that he be led to make comparisons between objects, to form judgments, to reason and to decide; and it is in the indefinite repetition of this exercise of attention and of intelligence that a real development ensues.

The series of objects to follow after the cylinders consists of three sets of geometrical solid forms:

(1) Ten wooden cubes colored pink. The sides of the cubes diminish from ten centimeters to one centimeter.

With these cubes the child builds a tower, first laying on the ground (upon a carpet) the largest cube, and then placing on the top of it all the others in their order of size to the very smallest. As soon as he has built the tower, the child, with a blow of his hand, knocks it down, so that the cubes are scattered on the carpet, and then he builds it up again.

(2) Ten wooden prisms, colored brown. The length of the prisms is twenty centimeters, and the square section diminishes from ten centimeters a side to the smallest, one centimeter a side.

The child scatters the ten pieces over a light-colored carpet, and then beginning sometimes with the thickest, sometimes with the thinnest, he places them in the right order of gradation upon a table.

(3) Ten rods, colored green, or alternately red and blue, all of which have the same square section of four centi-

meters a side, but vary by ten centimeters in length from ten centimeters to one meter.

The child scatters the ten rods on a large carpet and mixes them at random, and, by comparing rod with rod, he arranges them according to their order of length, so that they take the form of a set of organ pipes.

As usual, the teacher, by doing the exercises herself, first shows the child how the pieces of each set should be arranged, but it will often happen that the child learns, not directly from her, but by watching his companions. She will, however, always continue to watch the children, never losing sight of their efforts, and any correction of hers will be directed more toward preventing rough or disorderly use of the material than towards any *error* which the child may make in placing the rods in their order of gradation. The reason is that the mistakes which the child makes, by placing, for example, a small cube beneath one that is larger, are caused by his own lack of education, and it is the *repetition of the exercise* which, by refining his powers of observation, will lead him sooner or later to *correct himself*. Sometimes it happens that a child working with the long rods makes the most glaring mistakes. As the aim of the exercise, however, is *not* that the rods be arranged in the right order of gradation, but that the child *should practice by himself*, there is no need to intervene.

One day the child will arrange all the rods in their right order, and then, full of joy, he will call the teacher to come and admire them. The object of the exercise will thus be achieved.

These three sets, the cubes, the prisms, and the rods, cause the child to move about and to handle and carry objects which are difficult for him to grasp with his little hand. Again, by their use, he repeats the *training of the eye* to the recognition of differences of size between similar objects. The exercise would seem easier, from the sensory point of view, than the other with the cylinders described above.

As a matter of fact, it is more difficult, as there is *no control of the error in the material itself*. It is the child's eye alone which can furnish the control.

Hence the difference between the objects should strike the eye at once; for that reason larger objects are used, and the necessary visual power presupposes a previous preparation (provided for in the exercise with the solid insets).

During the same period the child can be doing other exercises. Among the material is to be found a small rectangular board, the surface of which is divided into two parts —rough and smooth. The child knows already how to wash his hands with cold water and soap; he then dries them and dips the tips of his fingers for a few seconds in tepid water. Graduated exercises for the thermic sense may also have their place here, as has been explained in my book *The Montessori Method*.

After this, the child is taught to pass the soft cushioned tips of his fingers *as lightly as possible* over the two separate surfaces, that he may appreciate their difference. The delicate *movement* backward and forward of the suspended hand, as it is brought into light contact with the surface, is an excellent exercise in control. The little hand, which has just been cleansed and given its tepid bath, gains much in grace and beauty, and the whole exercise is the first step in the education of the "tactile sense," which holds such an important place in my method.

When initiating the child into the education of the sense of touch, the teacher must always take an active part the first time; not only must she show the child "how it is done," her interference is a little more definite still, for she takes hold of his hand and guides it to touch the surfaces with the fingertips in the lightest possible way. She will make no explanations; her words will be rather to *encourage* the child with his hand to perceive the different sensations.

When he has perceived them, it is then that he repeats

the act by himself in the delicate way which he has been taught.

After the board with the two contrasting surfaces, the child is offered another board on which are gummed strips of paper which are rough or smooth in different degrees.

Graduated series of sandpaper cards are also given. The child perfects himself by exercises in touching these surfaces, not only refining his capacity for perceiving tactile differences which are always growing more similar, but also perfecting the movement of which he is ever gaining greater mastery.

Following these is a series of materials of every kind: velvets, satins, silks, woolens, cottons, coarse and fine linens. There are two similar pieces of each kind of material, and they are of bright and vivid colors.

The child is now taught a new movement. Where before he had to *touch*, he must now *feel* the materials, which, according to the degree of fineness or coarseness from coarse cotton to fine silk, are felt with movements correspondingly decisive or delicate. The child whose hand is already practiced finds the greatest pleasure in feeling the stuffs, and, almost instinctively, in order to enhance his appreciation of the tactile sensation he closes his eyes. Then, to spare himself the exertion, he blindfolds himself with a clean handkerchief, and as he feels the materials, he arranges the similar pieces in pairs, one upon the other, then, taking off the handkerchief, he ascertains for himself whether he has made any mistake.

This exercise in *touching* and *feeling* is peculiarly attractive to the child, and induces him to seek similar experiences in his surroundings. A little one, attracted by the pretty material of a visitor's dress, will be seen to go and wash his hands, then to come and touch the garment again and again with infinite delicacy, his face meanwhile expressing his pleasure and interest.

A little later we shall see the children interest themselves in a much more difficult exercise.

There are some little rectangular tablets which form part of the material. The tablets, though of identical size, are made of wood of varying qualities, so that they differ in weight and, through the property of the wood, in color also.

The child has to take a tablet and rest it delicately on the inner surfaces of his four fingers, spreading them well out. This will be another opportunity of teaching delicate movements.

The hand must move up and down as though to weigh the object, but the movement must be as imperceptible as possible. These little movements should diminish as the capacity and attention for perceiving the weight of the object becomes more acute and the exercise will be perfectly performed when the child comes to perceive the weight almost without any movement of the hands. It is only by the repetition of the attempts that such a result can be obtained.

Once the children are initiated into it by the teacher, they blindfold their eyes and repeat by themselves these exercises of the *baric sense*. For example, they lay the heavier wooden tablets on the right and the lighter on the left.

When the child takes off the handkerchief, he can see by the color of the pieces of wood if he has made a mistake.

A long time before this difficult exercise, and during the period when the child is working with the three sorts of geometrical solids and with the rough and smooth tablets, he can be exercising himself with a material which is very attractive to him.

This is the set of tablets covered with bright silk of shaded colors. The set consists of two separate boxes each containing sixty-four colors; that is, eight different tints, each of which has eight shades carefully graded. The first exercise for the child is that of *pairing the colors*; that is, he selects from a mixed heap of colors the two tablets which are alike, and lays them out, one beside the other. The teacher naturally does not offer the child all the one hundred and twenty-eight tablets in a heap, but chooses only a few of the brighter colors, for example, red, blue and yellow, and prepares and mixes up three or four pairs. Then, taking one tablet—perhaps the red one—she indicates to the child that he is to choose its counterpart from the heap. This done, the teacher lays the pair together on the table. Then she takes perhaps the blue and the child selects the tablet to form another pair. The teacher then mixes the tablets again for the child to repeat the exercise by himself, *i.e.*, to select the two red tablets, the two blue, the two yellow, etc., and to place the two members of each pair next to one another.

Then the couples will be increased to four or five, and little children of three years old end by pairing of their own accord ten or a dozen couples of mixed tablets.

When the child has given his eye sufficient practice in recognizing the identity of the pairs of colors, he is offered the shades of one color only, and he exercises himself in the perception of the slightest differences of shade in every color. Take, for example, the blue series. There are eight tablets in graduated shades. The teacher places them one beside another, beginning with the darkest, with the sole object of making the child understand "what is to be done."

She then leaves him alone to the interesting attempts which he spontaneously makes. It often happens that the child makes a mistake. If he has understood the idea and makes a mistake, it is a sign that *he has not yet reached the stage* of perceiving the differences between the graduations of one color. It is practice which perfects in the child that capacity for distinguishing the fine differences, and so we leave him alone to his attempts!

There are two suggestions that we can make to help him.

The first is that he should always select the darkest color from the pile. This suggestion greatly facilitates his choice by giving it a constant direction.

Secondly, we can lead him to observe from time to time any two colors that stand next to each other in order to compare them directly and apart from the others. In this way the child does not place a tablet without a particular and careful comparison with its neighbor.

Finally, the child himself will love to mix the sixty-four colors and then to arrange them in eight rows of pretty shades of color with really surprising skill. In this exercise also the child's hand is educated to perform fine and delicate movements and his mind is afforded special training in attention. He must not take hold of the tablets anyhow, he must avoid touching the colored silk, and must handle the tablets instead by the pieces of wood at the top and bottom. To arrange the tablets next to one another in a straight line at exactly the same level, so that the series looks like a beautiful shaded ribbon, is an act which demands a manual skill only obtained after considerable practice.

These exercises of the chromatic sense lead, in the case of the older children, to the development of the "color memory." A child having looked carefully at a color, is then invited to look for its companion in a mixed group of colors, without, of course, keeping the color he has observed under his eye to guide him. It is, therefore, by his memory that he recognizes the color, which he no longer compares with a reality but with an image impressed upon his mind.

The children are very fond of this exercise in "color memory"; it makes a lively digression for them, as they run with the image of a color in their minds and look for its corresponding reality in their surroundings. It is a real triumph for them to identify the idea with the corresponding reality and to *hold in their hands* the proof of the mental power they have acquired.

Another interesting piece of material is a little cabinet containing six drawers placed one above another. When they are opened they display six square wooden "frames" in each.

Almost all the frames have a large geometrical figure inserted in the center, each colored blue and provided with a small button for a handle. Each drawer is lined with blue paper, and when the geometrical figure is removed, the bottom is seen to reproduce exactly the same form.

The geometrical figures are arranged in the drawers according to analogy of form.

(1) In one drawer there are six circles decreasing in diameter.

(2) In another there is a square, together with five rectangles in which the length is always equal to the side of the square while the breadth gradually decreases.

(3) Another drawer contains six triangles, which vary either according to their sides or according to their angles (the equilateral, isosceles, scalene, right angled, obtuse angled, and acute angled).

(4) In another drawer there are six regular polygons containing from five to ten sides, i.e., the pentagon, hexagon, heptagon, octagon, nonagon, and decagon.

(5) Another drawer contains various figures: an oval, an ellipse, a rhombus, and a trapezoid.

(6) Finally, there are four plain wooden tablets, i.e., without any geometrical inset, which should have no button fixed to them; also two other irregular geometrical figures.

Connected with this material there is a wooden frame furnished with a kind of rack which opens like a lid, and serves, when shut, to keep firmly in place six of the insets which may be arranged on the bottom of the frame itself, entirely covering it.

This frame is used for the preparation of the *first presentation* to the child of the plane geometrical forms.

The teacher may select according to her own judgment certain forms from among the whole series at her disposal.

At first it is advisable to show the child only a few figures which differ very widely from one another in form. The next step is to present a larger number of figures, and after this to present consecutively figures more and more similar in form.

The first figures to be arranged in the frame will be, for example, the circle and the equilateral triangle, or the circle, the triangle and the square. The spaces which are left should be covered with the tablets of plain wood. Gradually the frame is completely filled with figures; first, with very dissimilar figures, as, for example, a square, a very narrow rectangle, a triangle, a circle, an ellipse and a hexagon, or with other figures in combination.

Afterward the teacher's object will be to arrange figures similar to one another in the frame, as, for example, the set of six rectangles, six triangles, six circles, varying in size, etc.

This exercise resembles that of the cylinders. The insets are held by the buttons and taken from their places. They are then mixed on the table and the child is invited to put them back in their places. Here also the control of the error is in the *material,* for the figure cannot be inserted perfectly except when it is put in its own place. Hence a series of "experiments," of "attempts" which end in victory. The child is led to compare the various forms; to realize in a concrete way the differences between them when an inset wrongly placed will not go into the aperture. In this way he educates his eye to the *recognition of forms.*

The new movement of the hand which the child must coordinate is of particular importance. He is taught to *touch the outline of the geometrical figures* with the soft tips of the index and middle finger of the right hand, or of the left as well, if one believes in ambidexterity. The child is made to touch the outline, not only of the *inset,* but also of the corresponding aperture, and, only after *having touched* them, is he to put back the inset into its place.

The *recognition* of the form is rendered much easier in

A child watches intently while another performs an exercise in mathematics. Montessori says that "the best teachers for children are children themselves," and notes that they "like the company of another child much better than that of an adult."

Children repeat exercises that interest them, as with the little girl (above) practicing pouring. A boy (below) turns down an offer of assistance; washing the table is *his* project.

This blindfolded girl is feeling the geometrical solids to develop her tactile and stereognostic senses.

A blindfolded girl is matching pieces of material according to their "feel." Such an exercise helps to develop the sense of touch.

The Pink Tower (opposite). The pieces increase in dimension by 1 cm.; the smallest cube measures 1 cm per side, the largest measures 10 cm.

The Trinomial Cube.

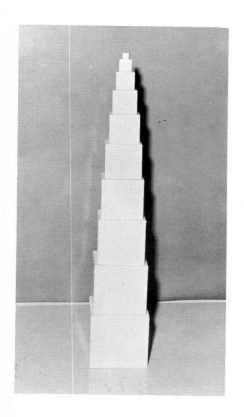

Children working with knobbed cylinders. This helps them develop thumb-finger dexterity in grasping.

Knobless colored cylinders (opposite); they correspond in dimension to the knobbed cylinders shown above. The child uses these to practice muscular coordination as he builds.

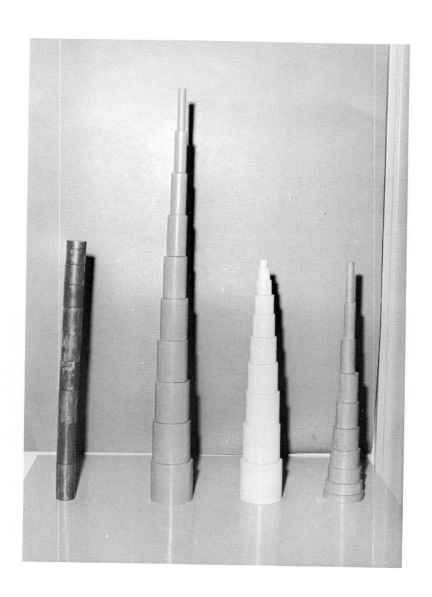

Numerical Rods stored on a shelf (above). Note the alternating dark and light colors for odd and even numbers. The equilateral triangles (below) are from one set of Constructive Triangles.

A child, working undisturbed on her own mat, is using one of the many trays from the Geometrical Cabinet.

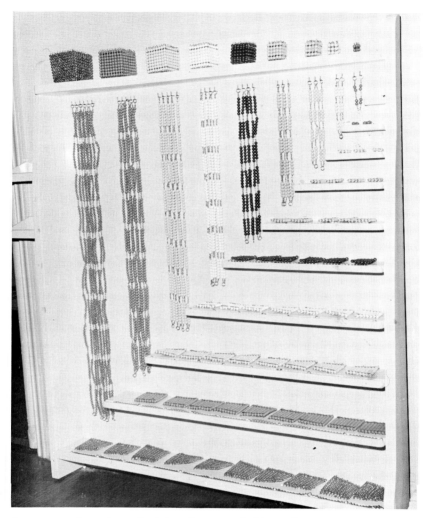

An array of mathematical bead material. The cube material is on the uppermost shelf; the square material is ranged on shelves below; and the linear chain material hangs in the middle. The famous 1,000-bead chain is on the extreme left.

An exercise in counting (above) using the bead material; and a six-year-old (below) doing subtraction (the "negative snake game") using the bead material.

A six-year-old (above) doing mathematics with the Bead Frame. The boy (below) has made a design on his paper with the metal inset, and is now coloring it. Note the orderly neatness of both workers.

Matching the name to the proper geometrical solid.

Material that can be used for long division.

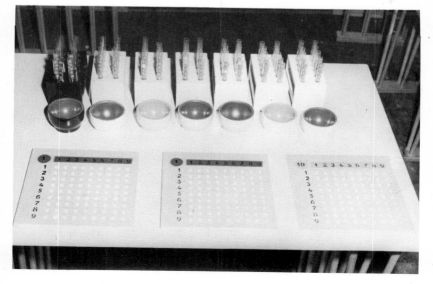

A four-and-a-half-year-old plays a tune on the bells while his brother, a year younger, works at the other end of the scale. The older boy already has a number of tunes at his command.

The Movable Alphabet (opposite) has many uses. In one exercise, the teacher says a word and the child chooses the letters to form the word.

Building words with the Movable Alphabet.

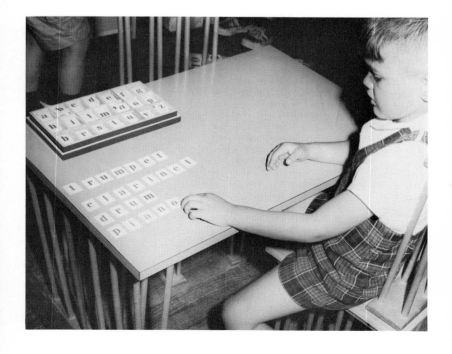

A child teaches himself geography (above) using special inset material. Similar didactic inset materials for learning biology (below) show the parts of a flower, a leaf and a tree. Preschool children enjoy learning biological nomenclature with such materials.

this way. Children who evidently do not *recognize the identities of form* by the eye and who make absurd attempts to place the most diverse figures one within the other, *do recognize* the forms after having touched their outlines, and arrange them very quickly in their right places.

The child's hand during this exercise of touching the outlines of the geometrical figures has a concrete guide in the object. This is especially true when he touches the frames, for his two fingers have only to follow the edge of the frame, which acts as an obstacle and is a very clear guide. The teacher must always intervene at the start to teach accurately this movement, which will have such an importance in the future. She must, therefore, show the child *how to touch*, not only by performing the movement herself slowly and clearly, but also by guiding the child's hand itself during his first attempts, so that he is sure to touch all the details— angles and sides. When his hand has learned to perform these movements with precision and accuracy, he will be *really* capable of following the outline of a geometrical figure, and through many repetitions of the exercise he will come to coordinate the movement *necessary* for the exact delineation of its form.

This exercise could be called an indirect but very real preparation for drawing. It is certainly the preparation of the hand to *trace an enclosed form*. The little hand which touches, feels, and knows how to follow a determined outline is preparing itself, without knowing it, for writing.

The children make a special point of touching the outlines of the plane insets with accuracy. They themselves have invented the exercise of blindfolding their eyes so as to recognize the forms by touch only, taking out and putting back the insets without seeing them.

Corresponding to every form reproduced in the plane insets there are three white cards square in shape and of exactly the same size as the wooden frames of the insets. These cards are kept in three special cardboard boxes, almost cubic in form.

On the cards are repeated, in three series, the same geometrical forms as those of the plane insets. The same measurements of the figures also are exactly reproduced.

In the first series the forms are filled in, *i.e.*, they are cut out in blue paper and gummed onto the card; in the second series there is only an outline about half a centimeter in width, which is cut out in the same blue paper and gummed to the card; in the third series, however, the geometrical figures are instead outlined only in black ink.

By the use of this second piece of the material, the exercise of the eye is gradually brought to perfection in the recognition of "plane forms." In fact, there is no longer the concrete control of error in the material as there was in the *wooden* insets, but the child, by his eye alone, must judge of identities of form when, instead of *fitting* the wooden forms into their corresponding apertures, he simply *rests* them on the cardboard figure.

Again, the refinement of the eye's power of discrimination increases every time the child passes from one series of cards to the next, and by the time that he has reached the third series, he can see the relation between a wooden object, which he holds in his hand, and an outline drawing; that is, he can connect the concrete reality with an *abstraction*. The *line* now assumes in his eyes a very definite meaning; and he accustoms himself to recognize, to interpret and to judge of forms contained by a simple outline.

The exercises are various; the children themselves invent them. Some love to spread out a number of the figures of the geometric insets before their eyes, and then, taking a handful of the cards and mixing them like playing cards, deal them out as quickly as possible, choosing the figures corresponding to the pieces. Then as a test of their choice, they place the wooden pieces upon the forms of the cards. At this exercise they often cover whole tables, putting the wooden figures above, and beneath each one in a vertical line, the three corresponding forms of the cardboard series.

Another game invented by the children consists in putting out and mixing all the cards of the three series on two or three adjoining tables. The child then takes a wooden geometrical form and places it, as quickly as possible, on the corresponding cards which he has recognized at a glance among all the rest.

Four or five children play this game together, and as soon as one of them has found, for example, the filled-in figure corresponding to the wooden piece, and has placed the piece carefully and precisely upon it, another child takes away the piece in order to place it on the same form in outline. The game is somewhat suggestive of chess.

Many children, without any suggestion from anyone, touch with the finger the outline of the figures in the three series of cards, doing it with seriousness of purpose, interest and perseverance.

We teach the children to name all the forms of the plane insets.

At first I had intended to limit my teaching to the most important names, such as square, rectangle, circle. But the children wanted to know all the names, taking pleasure in learning even the most difficult, such as trapezium, and decagon. They also show great pleasure in listening to the exact pronunciation of new words and in their repetition. Early childhood is, in fact, the age in which language is formed, and in which the sounds of a foreign language can be perfectly learned.

When the child has had long practice with the plane insets, he begins to make "discoveries" in his environment, recognizing forms, colors, and qualities already known to him—a result which, in general, follows after all the sensory exercises. Then it is that a great enthusiasm is aroused in him, and the world becomes for him a source of pleasure.

A little boy, walking one day alone on the roof terrace, repeated to himself with a thoughtful expression on his face, "The sky is blue! The sky is blue!" Once a cardinal, an admirer of the children of the school in Via Guisti, wished himself to bring them some biscuits and to enjoy the sight of a little greediness among the children. When he had finished his distribution, instead of seeing the children put the food hastily into their mouths, to his great surprise he heard them call out, "A triangle! A circle! A rectangle!" In fact, these biscuits were made in geometrical shapes.

In one of the people's dwellings at Milan, a mother, preparing the dinner in the kitchen, took from a packet a slice of bread and butter. Her little four-year-old boy who was with her said, "Rectangle." The woman going on with her work cut off a large corner of the slice of bread, and the child cried out, "Triangle!" She put this bit into the saucepan, and the child, looking at the piece that was left, called out more loudly than before, "And now it is a trapezium!"

The father, a workingman, who was present, was much impressed with the incident. He went straight to look for the teacher and asked for an explanation. Much moved, he said, "If I had been educated in that way I should not be now just an ordinary workman."

It was he who later on arranged for a demonstration to induce all the workmen of the dwellings to take an interest in the school. They ended by presenting the teacher with a parchment they had painted themselves, and on it, between the pictures of little children, they had introduced every kind of geometrical form.

As regards the touching of objects for the realization of their form, there is an infinite field of discovery open to the child in his environment. Children have been seen to stand opposite a beautiful pillar or a statue and, after having admired it, to close their eyes in a state of beatitude and pass their hands many times over the forms. One of our teachers met one day in a church two little brothers from the school in Via Guisti. They were standing looking at the small columns supporting the altar. Little by little the elder boy edged nearer the columns and began to touch them, then, as if he desired his little brother to share his pleasure, he drew him nearer and, taking his hand very gently, made him pass it round the smooth and beautiful shape of the column. But a sacristan came up at that moment and sent away "those tiresome children who were touching everything."

The great pleasure which the children derive from the recognition of *objects* by touching their form corresponds in itself to a sensory exercise.

Many psychologists have spoken of the *stereognostic* sense, that is, the capacity of recognizing forms by the movement of the muscles of the hand as it follows the outlines of solid objects. This sense does not consist only of the sense of touch, because the tactile sensation is only that by which we perceive the differences in quality of surfaces, rough or smooth. Perception of form comes from the combination of two sensations, tactile and muscular, muscular sensations being sensations of movement. What we call in the blind the *tactile* sense is in reality more often the stereognostic sense. That is, they perceive by means of their hands the *form of bodies*.

It is the special muscular sensibility of the child from three to six years of age who is forming his own muscular activity which stimulates him to use the stereognostic sense. When the child spontaneously blindfolds his eyes in order to recognize various objects, such as the plane and solid insets, he is exercising this sense.

There are many exercises which he can do to enable him to recognize with closed eyes objects of well-defined shapes, as, for example, the little bricks and cubes of Froebel, marbles, coins, beans, peas, etc. From a selection of different objects mixed together he can pick out those that are alike, and arrange them in separate heaps.

In the didactic material there are also geometrical solids—

pale blue in color—a sphere, a prism, a pyramid, a cone, a cylinder. The most attractive way of teaching a child to recognize these forms is for him to touch them with closed eyes and guess their names, the latter learned in a way which I will describe later. After an exercise of this kind the child when his eyes are open observes the forms with a much more lively interest. Another way of interesting him in the solid geometrical forms is to make them *move*. The sphere rolls in every direction; the cylinder rolls in one direction only; the cone rolls around itself; the prism and the pyramid, however, stand still, but the prism falls over more easily than the pyramid.

Little more remains of the didactic material for the education of the senses. There is, however, a series of six cardboard cylinders, either closed entirely or with wooden covers.

When these cases are shaken they produce sounds varying in intensity from loud to almost imperceptible sounds, according to the nature of the objects inside the cylinder.

There is a double set of these, and the exercise consists, first, in the recognition of sounds of equal intensity, arranging the cylinders in pairs. The next exercise consists in the comparison of one sound with another; that is, the child arranges the six cylinders in a series according to the loudness of sound which they produce. The exercise is analogous to that with the color spools, which also are paired and then arranged in gradation. In this case also the child performs the exercise seated comfortably at a table. After a preliminary explanation from the teacher he repeats the exercise by himself, his eyes being blindfolded that he may better concentrate his attention.

We may conclude with a general rule for the direction of the education of the senses. The order of procedure should be:

(1) Recognition of *identities* (the pairing of similar ob-

jects and the insertion of solid forms into places which fit them).

(2) Recognition of *contrasts* (the presentation of the extremes of a series of objects).

(3) Discrimination between objects very *similar* to one another.

To concentrate the attention of the child upon the sensory stimulus which is acting upon him at a particular moment, it is well, as far as possible, to *isolate* the sense; for instance, to obtain silence in the room for all the exercises and to blindfold the eyes for those particular exercises which do not relate to the education of the sense of sight.

The films give a general idea of all the sense exercises which the children can do with the material, and any one who has been initiated into the theory on which these are based will be able gradually to recognize them as they are seen practically carried out.

It is very advisable for those who wish to guide the children in these sensory exercises to begin, themselves, by working with the didactic material. The experience will give them some idea of what the children must feel, of the difficulties which they must overcome, etc., and, up to a certain point, it will give them some conception of the interest which these exercises can arouse in them. Whoever makes such experiments himself will be most struck by the fact that, when blindfolded, he finds that all the sensations of touch and hearing really appear more acute and more easily recognized. On account of this alone no small interest will be aroused in the experimenter.

Montessori and the Creative Arts

THE creative arts have a definite place within the Montessori curriculum. The very fact that painting, for example, appeals so to the young child is proof enough of his need for the freedom basic to creative self-expression. Every child has untapped creative potential to be nurtured within the prepared environment of the Montessori school, where he should be exposed to an understanding and creative teacher sufficiently trained and interested in the various art media.

Montessori notes that there are what she terms "sensitive periods" in the child's life for acquiring various skills, habits, and attitudes. This is true of the fine arts as well as other areas, such as language development. Although the various sensitive periods remain to be studied definitively, we know, for example, that the child from approximately two until four years of age displays a sensitive period for painting, drawing and other artistic activity. We can speculate that there may be various sensitive periods for the various art forms, their history, theory, and technique.

Artistic expression is especially good for those children who have been overstimulated to the point that the Montessori apparatus does not hold its usual appeal. For such children, art can be a first step along the path toward the other Montessori exercises; art can offer a therapeutic tranquillity that the child has sought in vain elsewhere.

Early training in art can develop all manner of cultural interests and appreciation. As man is increasingly faced with the challenge of wisely utilizing his mounting leisure time, art may appropriately become a never-ending source of personal fulfillment. Individual artistic accomplishment can help offset negative effects of standardization, automation and other conformity-producing aspects of our "prefabricated" style of life. What machine can ever match man's creative mentality?

Art education, involving as it does Montessori motor, sensory and "intellectual" components, can be integrated into the Montessori curriculum at all age levels, and with many subject areas, such as history and mathematics. Six-year-olds, for example, are perfectly capable of handling simple perspective. And why not let the youngster set up his own still life consisting of some colorful Montessori sensory apparatus? Art, potentially, is at least as important as any other aspect of early childhood education.

Media that the writer has found appealing to small children include "play dough," felt-tipped pens, charcoal, colored pencils, and watercolor sets. Tracing paper is also very popular, enabling the child to both copy and create, as it were, simultaneously. Here, the child will display his love of repetition, of which Montessori speaks, as he practices drawing a likeness. Work with tracing paper need not be construed as plagiaristic stifling of creativity. Rather, the practice in representation it provides reinforces the process of reality-learning in the young child.

All of these media should be carefully prepared for and properly introduced. Learning to hold and use a colored pencil, for example, is a skill; the acquisition of such a skill should not be left to chance. After mastering some of the media already mentioned, the child should be ready for easel work and tempera color. The first step, again, is to demonstrate to the child how to handle the tools and material. In the mixing of paints, for example, a definite sequence of steps facilitates the child's learning. The teacher can first explore with the child the possibilities of black—diluting it for transparency, using it in line, form, etc. This can be followed by adding white, then exploring the many possibilities of white combined with black.

The primary colors (red, blue, yellow) can be added one by one, with the teacher allowing the child always to discover through experimentation what color can (and very importantly) cannot do. She must understand her role as guardian of the child's spontaneity, permitting him to work with a minimum of restrictions while promoting the conditions necessary for concentration upon the creative task at hand.

In art the child has the opportunity to remove something from the abstract of his own understanding and place it within the concrete, translating mind into matter. The small child may find self-expression in an art form such as painting easier than in, say, writing prose, because of the differences in the "tools" and skills involved.

In a Montessori classroom, one may expect to find the children using many different media as their needs dictate. They show great interest in each other's efforts, which leads to much sharing and informal learning, and to respect for the individuality and originality of the work of others. But above all the child should be allowed to express his individuality himself.

Jo Ann T. Reddit, B.F.A.

MUSIC

With all this a way has been opened to a really musical education.

—*The Montessori Elementary Materials*, p. 363

Anna Maccheroni, a pupil of Montessori, and directress first of the "Children's House" in Milan and later of the one in the Franciscan Convent in Rome, was described by Montessori as "a gifted musician." According to Montessori,[1] it was she who invented and had manufactured the series of thirteen bells hung upon a wooden frame used in the Montessory classroom. However, in an interesting reference to a Maccheroni lecture she attended, Sheila Radice says:

> In the course of the lecture, Signorina Maccheroni said that people were often kind enough to ascribe the musical work in the Montessori Method to her, and that in return she could only say that she had been studying music for a long time before she met Dr. Montessori, but that it had never occurred to her to approach music in this way. She thanked the public, therefore, but would ask them to render unto Caesar the things that were Caesar's.[2]

Although there is ample opportunity in the Montessori curriculum for "free" expression with paints, clay, and other media, Montessori emphasizes the importance of sensory and motor education for the child as a foundation for creative endeavor. The child needs, for example, to learn to handle brushes, as well as to discriminate swiftly and precisely fine gradations of color.

Creativeness also involves a large measure of self-discipline. Montessori stresses the importance of allowing the young child to complete "cycles of activity." This involves selecting a task, working at it until mastery is achieved, and finally returning the materials used to their proper place. Such an opportunity to concentrate for relatively long periods of time upon attractive, useful, self-selected tasks, rarely afforded children in their usual environment, helps develop self-discipline and the habit of "seeing things through" to completion.

During his first days in a Montessori classroom, a child learns that every piece of material has its place. As he begins to move, work, and initiate activity on his own, after having seen the use of some materials demonstrated by the teacher, *he is ready to complete a "cycle of activity." The child knows he will find the material wanted in its particular place. He also knows that the material must be taken from the place where he found it and carried to where he is going to work with it. After the material is worked with, it must be replaced by him in the condition in which he found it in the place from which it was taken. This is a completed cycle of activity, and is an important aspect of the "learning how to learn" dynamics of the Montessori classroom.*

Selected References

[1] Montessori, Maria, *The Montessori Method*. London: Heinemann, 1912. P. 204.
[2] Radice, Sheila, *The New Children*. London: Hodder and Stroughton. Pp. 81-82.

EDUCATION OF THE AUDITORY AND MUSICAL SENSES

Today forty children can be seen walking as softly as possible during a tune played pianissimo. These same children on the day when they first heard the piano kept calling to the teacher, "Play louder; we cannot hear!" and yet at that time the teacher was playing not pianissimo, but mezzo forte!

—*The Montessori Elementary Materials*, p. 345

For the beginning of the education of the musical sense, we use in Rome . . . a double series of bells forming an octave with tones and semitones. These metal bells, which stand upon a wooden rectangular base, are all alike in appearance, but, when struck with a little wooden hammer, give out sounds corresponding to the notes doh, re, mi, fah, soh, lah, ti, doh, doh ♯, re ♯, fah ♯, soh ♯, lah ♯.

One series of bells is arranged in chromatic order upon a long board, upon which are painted rectangular spaces which are black and white and of the same size as the bases which support the bells. As on a pianoforte keyboard, the white spaces correspond to the tones, and the black to the semitones.

At first the only bells to be arranged upon the board are those which correspond to the tones; these are set upon the white spaces in the order of the musical notes, doh, re, mi, fah, soh, lah, ti, doh.

To perform the first exercise the child strikes with a small hammer the first note of the series already arranged (doh). Then among a second series of corresponding bells which, arranged without the semitones, are mixed together upon the table, he tries, by striking the bells one after the other, to find the sound which is the same as the first one he has struck (doh). When he has succeeded in finding the corresponding sound, he puts the bell thus chosen opposite the first one (doh) upon the board. Then he strikes the second bell, *re,* once or twice; then from among the mixed group of bells he makes experiments until he recognizes *re,* which he places opposite the second bell of the series already arranged. He continues in the same way right to the end, looking for the identity of the sounds and performing an exercise of *pairing* similar to that already done in the case of the sound boxes, the colors, etc.

Later, he learns in order the sounds of the musical scale, striking in rapid succession the bells arranged in order, and also accompanying his action with his voice—doh, re, mi, fah, soh, lah, ti, doh. When he is able to recognize and *remember* the series of sounds, the child takes the eight bells and, after mixing them up, he tries by striking them with the hammer, to find *doh,* then *re,* etc. Every time that he takes a new note, he strikes from the beginning all the bells already recognized and arranged in order—doh, *re*, doh re, *mi*; doh, re mi, *fah*; doh, re mi, fah, *soh*, etc. In this way he succeeds in arranging all the bells in the order of the scale, guided only by his ear, and having succeeded, he strikes all the notes one after the other up and down the scale. This exercise fascinates children from five years old upward.

If the objects which have been described constitute the didactic material for the beginnings of a methodical education of the auditory sense, I have no desire to limit to them an educational process which is so important and already so complex in its practice, whether in the long-established methods of treatment for the deaf, or in modern physiological musical education. In fact, I also use resonant metal tubes, small bars of wood which emit musical notes, and strings (little harps), upon which the children seek to recognize the tones they have already learned with the exercise of the bells. The pianoforte may also be used for the same purpose. In this way the difference in *timbre* comes to be perceived together with the differences in tone. At the same time various exercises, already mentioned, such as the marches played on the piano for rhythmic exercises, and the simple songs sung by the children themselves, offer extensive means for the development of the musical sense.

To quicken the child's attention in special relation to sounds there is a most important exercise which, contrary to all attempts made up to this time in the practice of education, consists not in producing but in eliminating, as far as possible, all sounds from the environment. My "lesson of silence" has been very widely applied, even in schools where the rest of my method has not found its way, for the sake of its practical effect upon the discipline of the children.

The children are taught "not to move"; to inhibit all those motor impulses which may arise from any cause whatsoever, and in order to induce in them real "immobility," it is necessary to initiate them in the *control* of all their movements. The teacher, then, does not limit herself to saying, "Sit still," but she gives them the example herself, showing them how to sit absolutely still; that is, with feet still, body still, arms still, head still. The respiratory movements should also be performed in such a way as to produce no sound.

The children must be taught how to succeed in this exercise. The fundamental condition is that of finding a comfortable position, *i.e.*, a position of equilibrium. As they are seated for this exercise, they must therefore make themselves comfortable either in their little chairs or on the ground. When immobility is obtained, the room is half-darkened, or else the children close their eyes, or cover them with their hands.

It is quite plain to see that the children take a great interest in the "Silence"; they seem to give themselves up to a kind of spell: they might be said to be wrapped in meditation. Little by little, as each child, watching himself, becomes more and more still, the silence deepens till it becomes absolute and can be felt, just as the twilight gradually deepens while the sun is setting.

Then it is that slight sounds, unnoticed before, are heard: the ticking of the clock, the chirp of a sparrow in the garden, the flight of a butterfly. The world becomes full of imperceptible sounds which invade that deep silence without disturbing it, just as the stars shine out in the dark sky without banishing the darkness of the night. It is almost the discovery of a new world where there is rest. It is, as it were, the twilight of the world of loud noises and of the uproar that oppresses the spirit. At such a time the spirit is set free and opens out like the corolla of the convolvulus.

And leaving metaphor for the reality of facts, can we not all recall feelings that have possessed us at sunset, when all the vivid impressions of the day, the brightness and clamor, are silenced? It is not that we miss the day, but that our spirit expands. It becomes more sensitive to the inner play of emotions, strong and persistent, or changeful and serene.

> It was that hour when mariners feel longing
> And hearts grow tender.
>
> (Dante, trans. Longfellow)

The lesson of silence ends with a general calling of the children's names. The teacher, or one of the children, takes her place behind the class or in an adjoining room, and "calls" the motionless children, one by one, by name; the call is made in a whisper, that is, without vocal sound. This demands a close attention on the part of the child, if he is to hear his name. When his name is called he must rise and find his way to the voice which called him; his movements must be light and vigilant, and so controlled *as to make no noise.*

When the children have become acquainted with *silence,* their hearing is in a manner refined for the perception of sounds. Those sounds which are too loud become gradually displeasing to the ear of one who has known the pleasure of silence, and has discovered the world of delicate sounds. From this point the children gradually go on to perfect themselves; they walk lightly, take care not to knock against the furniture, move their chairs without noise, and place things upon the table with great care. The result of this is seen in the grace of carriage and of movement, which is especially delightful on account of the way in which it has been brought about. It is not a grace taught externally for the sake of beauty or regard for the world, but one which is born of the pleasure felt by the spirit in immobility and silence. The soul of the child wishes to free itself from the irksomeness of sounds that are too loud, from obstacles to its peace during work. These children, with the grace of pages to a noble lord, are serving their spirits.

This exercise develops very definitely the social spirit. No other lesson, no other "situation," could do the same. A profound silence can be obtained even when more than fifty children are crowded together in a small space, provided that *all* the children know how to keep still and want to do it; but one disturber is enough to take away the charm.

Here is demonstration of the cooperation of all the members of a community to achieve a common end. The children gradually show increased power of *inhibition*; many of them, rather than disturb the silence, refrain from brushing a fly off the nose, or suppress a cough or sneeze. The same exhibition of collective action is seen in the care with which the children move to avoid making a noise during their work. The lightness with which they run on tiptoe, the grace with which they shut a cupboard, or lay an object on the table, these are qualities that must be *acquired by all,* if the environment is to become tranquil and free from disturbance. One rebel is sufficient to mar this achievement; one noisy child, walking on his heels or banging the door, can disturb the peaceful atmosphere of the small community.

THE READING OF MUSIC

It is no wonder that reading is one of the rocks on which the rudderless ship of elementary education inevitably runs aground.

—*The Montessori Elementary Materials,* p. 175

The Reading of Music

When the child knows how to read, he can make a first application of this knowledge to the reading of the names of musical notes.

In connection with the material for sensory education, consisting of the series of bells, we use a didactic material, which serves as an introduction to musical reading. For this purpose we have, in the first place, a wooden board, not very long, and painted pale green. On this board the staff is cut out in black, and in every line and space are cut round holes, inside each of which is written the name of the note in its reference to the treble clef.

There is also a series of little white discs which can be fitted into the holes. On one side of each disc is written the name of the note (doh, re, mi, fah, soh, lah, ti, doh).

The child, guided by the name written on the discs, puts them, with the name uppermost, in their right places on the board and then reads the names of the notes. This exercise he can do by himself, and he learns the position of each note on the staff. Another exercise which the child can do at the same time is to place the disc bearing the name of the note on the rectangular base of the corresponding bell, whose sound he has already learned to recognize by ear in the sensorial exercise described above.

Following this exercise there is another staff made on a board of green wood, which is longer than the other and has neither indentures nor signs. A considerable number of discs, on one side of which are written the names of the notes, is at the disposal of the child. He takes up a disc at random, reads its name and places it on the staff, with the name underneath, so that the white face of the disc shows on the top. By the repetition of this exercise the child is enabled to arrange many discs on the same line or in the same space. When he has finished, he turns them all over so that the names are outside, and so finds out if he has made mistakes. After learning the treble clef the child passes on to learn the bass with great ease.

To the staff described above can be added another similar to it. The child beginning with *doh*, lays the discs on the board in ascending order in their right position until the octave is reached: doh, re, mi, fah, soh, lah, ti, doh. Then he descends the scale in the same way, returning to *doh*, but continuing to place the discs always to the right: soh, fah, mi, re, doh. In this way he forms an angle. At this point he descends again to the lower staff, ti, lah, soh, fah, mi, re, doh, then he ascends again on the other side: re, mi, fah, soh, lah, ti, and by forming with his two lines of discs another angle in the bass, he has completed a rhombus, "the rhombus of the notes."

After the discs have been arranged in this way, the upper staff is separated from the lower. In the lower the notes are arranged according to the bass clef. In this way the first elements of musical reading are presented to the child, reading which corresponds to *sounds* with which the child's ear is already acquainted.

For a first practical application of this knowledge we have used in our schools a miniature pianoforte keyboard, which reproduces the essentials of this instrument, although in a simplified form, and so that they are visible. Two octaves only are reproduced, and the keys, which are small, are proportioned to the hand of a little child of four or five years, as the keys of the common piano are proportioned to those of the adult. All the mechanism of the key is visible. On striking a key one sees the hammer rise, on which is written the name of the note. The hammers are black and white, like the notes.

With this instrument it is very easy for the child to practice alone, finding the notes on the keyboard corresponding to some bar of written music, and following the movements of the fingers made in playing the piano.

The keyboard in itself is mute, but a series of resonant tubes, resembling a set of organ pipes, can be applied to the upper surface, so that the hammers striking these produce musical notes corresponding to the keys struck. The child can then pursue his exercises with the control of the musical sounds.

IV

INTELLECTUAL EDUCATION

Each subject of study, as, for instance, arithmetic, grammar, geometry, natural science, music, literature, should be presented by means of external objects upon a well-defined systematic plan.

—*Spontaneous Activity in Education,* p. 85

Beginnings of a Theory
Behind Montessori

THERE can be no doubt today that the Montessori educational approach is a success. Thriving schools abound in this country and elsewhere, and are constantly growing in numbers. We must not, however, be content with mere facts. We must seek to rationalize these facts and to appreciate the underlying principles that make them possible.

It may seem to many that the pursuit of theory is idle, but actually the exclusive and inordinate pursuit of immediate goals, without regard for theory, is destructive. One is inclined to think of what a nest of caterpillars, each seeking its immediate purpose, can do to a tree. There is need of the perspective of a horticulturist to make the tree grow optimally. And so it is with educational facts; there is need of a theoretical overview to help make them evolve further.

It is the distinct impression of many that Montessori thinking has largely been concerned with facts or, at best, with molecular theories. There is need of a comprehensive point of view that can give meaning and fertility to the entire process. A theoretical perspective that promises to be fruitful in providing adequate underpinning for Montessori thought is Dr. Donald O. Hebb's neuropsychological theory. Montessori stresses experience, sensation, social interaction, the cultivation of usefulness, a general awareness of the physical environment, the progressive discovery of meaning, and many other related educational methods. By studying the basic assumptions of Hebb's theory we can arrive at an explanation for the adaptiveness of Montessori's methods.

119

At the heart of Hebb's theory is the realization that stimuli offered to children should be spread in both intensity and extension. Hebb's theory calls for simultaneous appeal to several sensory dimensions. It suggests that tasks be adjusted to the factor of incomplete neurological development. When the adjustment is made, learning progresses more quickly. What is required is organized stimulation geared to the neuropsychological maturity level of the child. There are numerous illustrations that could be given; for example, it has been shown that fashioning a pen or pencil to fit a child's hand more perfectly has increased writing speed. Hebb's theory also suggests that it is appropriate to anticipate to some measure a child's learning experience with preliminary or preparatory tasks. One must challenge the child. He must be expected to stand on tiptoe periodically, in order to reach for the highest possible achievement goals. He must be stimulated and motivated; if we leave him to his own resources in an impoverished environment, we have no reason to wonder about his becoming a so-called learning difficulty.

On the whole, children tend to do what they can. If they receive sensitive assistance from parents, they learn more, and they learn earlier. Hebb's theory clearly stresses the importance of annexing kinesthesis with virtually all early childhood learning. When a child does something about an object, he senses it more clearly and is likely to utilize it more spontaneously in problem-solving behavior.

Another major point of significance is that children's experiences must cover all possible features that are within their capacity to comprehend. The learning of the future for them will be extremely complex, but the basic building blocks will be the primitive learning of childhood. These perspectives must encompass as much as possible of their environment, so that they can be more adequately prepared for the acquisition of advanced knowledge. Why shouldn't a child start a game with a jet-age "countdown" instead of "1, 2, 3, go"?

Adolescent and adult schooling will be replete with symbolization. Therefore, the symbols must be firmly established early, and must be as numerous as possible. With an abundant supply of solid building blocks, the child can hopefully anticipate an adult structure of scientific concepts.

In substance, Hebb's theoretical approach starts from a rich exploration of the sensory world in order to prepare the child for the learning tasks of maturity. Actually, he dips into neurological findings to support his theory. His assumptions are intricate, and perhaps somewhat removed from facts. However, his organization of thought from the "cell assemblies" up to the most complex superordinate perceptual structures, merges at the practical level with the Montessori recipe. If there were more consciousness of the system that Hebb derived and others have elaborated, there might well be even more "cooking" in the Montessori classroom.

E. PAUL BENOIT, PH.D.

LANGUAGE, VOCABULARY AND KNOWLEDGE OF THE WORLD

Many defects which become permanent, such as speech defects, the child acquires through being neglected during the most important period of his age, the period between three and six, at which time he forms and establishes his principal functions.

—*The Montessori Method*, p. 45

Montessori effectively links language development *with* sensory education, *one facilitating the other. The coin of the child's realm, culturally, is language, which comes to signify how he feels, what he is doing and the objects with which he is working. He must learn to associate the appropriate word with a particular sensation, action, or form, in order to organize his percepts and concepts. The Montessori teacher, with individual lessons, helps the child to gain a precise vocabulary for form, dimension, and gradation.*

The "sensitive period" for language learning is during the first six years of the child's life. This is the "ripe" time neurologically and pedagogically to master the mother tongue and a second language. It is also the time to introduce the child to the nomenclature of various subjects— geography, geometry, etc. The child trained to observe, label, and classify in the Montessori environment is prepared to cope perceptually with the stimuli of the environment at large, organizing his experiences and discovering relationships as he classifies his concepts to develop an ordered or "prepared" mind.

Neurologist Wilder Penfield, referring to the experiences of his own children, notes that a child exposed early enough to three languages instead of one learns the units of all three without added effort or confusion. When a child takes up a new language for the first time in the second decade of life, past the "ideal time for language beginning," it will be difficult to achieve a good result "because it is unphysiological."[1]

Norbert Wiener, the founder of cybernetics and himself a preschool reader, describes speech in The Human Use of Human Beings *as "the greatest interest and most distinctive achievement of man," and mentions "a critical period during which speech is most readily learned." Speech, he feels, is so important to normal social life that if it is not learned at the proper time "the whole social aspect of the individual will be aborted."[2]*

Ernst Cassirer, in An Essay On Man, *mentions the "hunger for names" which appears in every normal child at a certain age, and which signals the child's desire for "the detection and conquest of an objective world."[3] Human language has been described by Julian Huxley as "the most complicated kind of skill in existence,"[4] and by Allison Davis and Robert Havighurst as "the most complex of human learning."[5] Yet the normal child by age four displays an amazing facility in receptive and expressive language. Alfred North Whitehead speaks of the "miracle" of the child's achievement in mastering language.[6]*

Selected References

[1] Penfield, Wilder, and Lamar Roberts, *Speech and Brain-Mechanisms.* Princeton University Press, 1959. See pp. 253-255, "Language Learning by the Direct Method."

[2] Wiener, Norbert, *The Human Use of Human Beings.* Boston: Houghton Mifflin, 1950. P. 95.

[3] Cassirer, Ernst, *An Essay On Man.* New Haven, Connecticut: Yale University Press, Second Printing, May, 1962. Pp. 132-133.

[4] Huxley, Julian, *Evolution in Action.* London: Chatto and Windus, 1953. P. 109.

[5] Davis, Allison, and Robert Havighurst, *Father of the Man: How Your Child Get His Personality.* Boston: Houghton Mifflin, 1947. P. 107.

[6] Whitehead, Alfred North, *The Aims of Education and Other Essays.* New York: New American Library, 1949. Pp. 27-28.

Language, Vocabulary and Knowledge of the World

The special importance of the sense of hearing comes from the fact that it is the sense organ connected with speech. Therefore, to train the child's attention to follow sounds and noises which are produced in the environment, to recognize them and to discriminate between them, is to prepare his attention to follow more accurately the sounds of articulate language. The teacher must be careful to pronounce clearly and completely the sounds of the word when she speaks to a child, even though she may be speaking in a low voice, almost as if telling him a secret. The children's songs are also a good means for obtaining exact pronunciation. The teacher, when she teaches them, pronounces slowly, separating the component sounds of the word pronounced.

But a special opportunity for training in clear and exact speech occurs when the lessons are given in the nomenclature relating to the sensory exercises. In every exercise, when the child has *recognized* the differences between the qualities of the objects, the teacher fixes the idea of this quality with a word. Thus, when the child has many times built and rebuilt the tower of the pink cubes, at an opportune moment the teacher draws near him, and taking the two extreme cubes, the largest and the smallest, and showing them to him, says, "This is large"; "This is small." The two words only, *large* and *small,* are pronounced several times in succession with strong emphasis and with a very clear pronunciation, "This is *large,* large, large"; after which there is a moment's pause. Then the teacher, to see if the child has understood, verifies with the following tests: "Give me the large one. Give me the *small* one." Again, "The large one." "Now the small one." "Give me the large one." Then there is another pause. Finally, the teacher, pointing to the objects in turn asks, "What is this?" The child, if he has learned, replies rightly, "Large," "Small." The teacher then urges the child to repeat the words always more clearly and as accurately as possible. "What is it?" "Large." "What?" "Large." "Tell me nicely, what is it?" "Large."

Large and *small* objects are those which differ only in size and not in form; that is, all three dimensions change more or less proportionally. We should say that a house is "large" and a hut is "small." When two pictures represent the same objects in different dimensions one can be said to be an enlargement of the other.

When, however, only the dimensions referring to the section of the object change, while the length remains the same, the objects are respectively "thick" and "thin." We should say of two posts of equal height, but different cross section, that one is "thick" and the other is "thin." The teacher, therefore, gives a lesson on the brown prisms similar to that with the cubes in the three "periods" which I have described:

Period 1. *Naming.* "This is thick. This is thin."

Period 2. *Recognition.* "Give me the *thick*. Give me the *thin*."

Period 3. *The Pronunciation of the Word.* "What is this?"

There is a way of helping the child to recognize differences in dimension and to place the objects in correct gradation. After the lesson which I have described, the teacher scatters the brown prisms, for instance, on a carpet, says to the child, "Give me the thickest of all," and lays the object on a table. Then, again, she invites the child to look for *the thickest* piece among those scattered on the floor, and every time the piece chosen is laid in its order on the table next to the piece previously chosen. In this way the child accustoms himself always to look either for the *thickest* or the *thinnest* among the rest, and so has a guide to help him to lay the pieces in gradation.

When there is one dimension only which varies, as in the case of the rods, the objects are said to be "long" and "short," the varying dimension being length. When the varying dimension is height, the objects are said to be "tall" and "short"; when the breadth varies, they are "broad" and "narrow."

Of these three varieties we offer the child as a fundamental lesson only that in which the *length* varies, and we teach the differences by means of the usual "three periods," and by asking him to select from the pile at one time always the "longest," at another always the "shortest."

The child in this way acquires great accuracy in the use of words. One day the teacher had ruled the blackboard with very fine lines. A child said, "What small lines!" "They are not small," corrected another. "They are *thin*."

When the names to be taught are those of colors or of forms, so that it is not necessary to emphasize contrast between extremes, the teacher can give more than two names at the same time, as, for instance, "This is red." "This is blue." "This is yellow." Or, again, "This is a square." "This is a triangle." "This is a circle." In the case of a *gradation,* however, the teacher will select (if she is teaching the colors) the two extremes "dark" and "light," then making choice always of the "darkest" and the "lightest."

Many of the lessons here described can be seen in the films; lessons on touching the plane insets and the surfaces, in walking on the line, in color memory, in the nomenclature relating to the cubes and the long rods, in the composition of words, reading, writing, etc.

By means of these lessons the child comes to know many words very thoroughly—large, small; thick, thin; long, short; dark, light; rough, smooth; heavy, light; hot, cold; and the names of many colors and geometrical forms. Such words do not relate to any particular *object,* but to a psychic acquisition on the part of the child. In fact, the name is given *after a long exercise,* in which the child, concentrating his attention on different qualities of objects, has made comparisons, reasoned, and formed judgments, until he has acquired a power of discrimination which he did not possess before. In a word, he has *refined his senses*; his observation of things has been thorough and fundamental; he has *changed himself.*

He finds himself, therefore, facing the world with *psychic* qualities refined and quickened. His powers of observation and of recognition have greatly increased. Further, the mental images which he has succeeded in establishing are not a confused medley; they are all classified—forms are distinct from dimensions, and dimensions are classed according to the qualities which result from the combinations of varying dimensions.

All these are quite distinct from *gradations.* Colors are divided according to tint and to richness of tone, silence is distinct from non-silence, noises from sounds, and everything has its own exact and appropriate name. The child then has not only developed in himself special qualities of observation and of judgment, but the objects which he observes may be said to go into their place according to the order established in his mind, and they are placed under their appropriate name in an exact classification.

Does not the student of the experimental sciences prepare himself in the same way to observe the outside world? He may find himself like the uneducated man in the midst of the most diverse natural objects, but he differs from the uneducated man in that he has *special qualities* for observation. If he is a worker with the microscope, his eyes are trained to see in the range of the microscope certain minute details which the ordinary man cannot distinguish. If he is an astronomer, he will look through the same telescope as the curious visitor or *dilettante,* but he will see much more clearly. The same plants surround the botanist and the ordinary wayfarer, but the botanist sees in every plant those qualities which are classified in his mind, and assigns to each plant its own place in the natural orders, giving it its exact name. It is this capacity for recognizing a plant in a complex order of classification which distinguishes the botanist from the ordinary gardener, and it is *exact* and scientific language which characterizes the trained observer.

Now, the scientist who has developed special qualities of observation and who "possesses" an order in which to classify external objects will be the man to make scientific *discoveries*. It will never be he who, without preparation and order, wanders dreaming among plants or beneath the starlit sky.

In fact, our little ones have the impression of continually "making discoveries" in the world about them; and in this they find the greatest joy. They take from the world a knowledge which is ordered and inspires them with enthusiasm. Into their minds there enters "the Creation" instead of "the Chaos"; and it seems that their souls find therein a divine exultation.

Montessori and Early
Intellectual Education

IN the light of contemporary educational theory, one of the most remarkable features of the Montessori method is its emphasis on the early development of the language arts, including reading and writing. For, within the decade 1955–1965, several leaders in psychology and related disciplines began to experiment with the introduction of reading and writing to the child between the ages of three and six.

This new interest contrasts strongly with a previous period of some forty years during which the early exposure of the child to reading and writing was deliberately discouraged; indeed, on a popular level it still often is. Yet, in the first decade of this century Montessori advocated and successfully accomplished the mastery of reading and writing skills in her students before they reached the age of six. It has taken many years for her work to receive the attention it warrants, but today the careful efforts of researchers are proving that her ideas and methods have revolutionary implications for the teaching of the language arts.

Recently J. McV. Hunt, a leading student of the development of intelligence in animals and humans, wrote that he had found in the Montessori Method a practical solution for unlocking the full intellectual potentials of the child.[1] Nor is Hunt alone in his recognition of the importance of early learning. The names of the scholars and scientists who have reopened the issue of intellectual education before age six include some of the most prominent people in psychology and education. Jerome S. Bruner, B. F. Skinner, O. K. Moore, William Fowler, Arthur W. Staats, Nancy M. Rambusch, Donald Hebb, Dolores Durkin, and Benjamin S. Bloom have all within the past few years published articles, books, and research studies which elevate the question of early education to a position of central concern in learning theory.

Many of these students of learning theory have already begun to successfully experiment with the programming of reading instruction in the preschool period. Arthur W. Staats, of Arizona State University, has been investigating language development in children. In a recent experiment he demonstrated that four-year-old children could be taught to read in a situation where each child was given individual attention and opportunity to learn at his own rate.[2] William Fowler, a Yale psychologist, taught his two-year-old daughter to read. He published his findings in a monograph in which he reviews the scientific evidence that favors early intellectual stimulation of the child.[3]

In 1962, Dolores Durkin published a key study demonstrating the value of early reading experience. Durkin followed fifty preschool readers for eight years. All were taught to read, to some extent, before the age of six. After three years of school, all showed evidence of having profited from the early reading. When the early readers were compared with children of equivalent IQ it was shown that the early readers had made greater progress in school.[4]

B. F. Skinner, the modern exponent of teaching machines, and the major learning theorist in behavioristic psychology, recently suggested that reading should be started in the nursery with programmed instruction.[5] Omar K. Moore, of Yale University, has been teaching children as young as three to read. He has developed an auto-instructional reading program using a special electric typewriter. Moore has discovered that children will largely teach themselves if given the proper equipment and opportunity to work at an individual rate. The early development of intellectual skills such as reading and writing has become a subject of major concern during the present period. Yet, Maria Montessori developed concepts and classroom practices which actually produced "early readers" among the underprivileged children of an Italian slum more than half a century ago.

GEORGE L. STEVENS, M.A.

Selected References

[1] Montessori, Maria, *The Montessori Method*. New York: Schocken, 1964. P. xxix (Introduction by J. McV. Hunt).

[2] Staats, Arthur, "The Conditioning of Textual Responses Using Extrinsic Reinforcers." *Journal of the Experimental Analysis of Behavior*, V, January, 1962.

[3] Fowler, William, "Teaching a Two-year-old to Read: An Experiment in Early Childhood Education." *Genetic Psychology Monographs*, 1962.

[4] Durkin, Dolores, "Children Who Learned to Read at Home." *Elementary School Journal*, LXII, October, 1961, pp. 15-18.

[5] Skinner, B. F., "Why We Need Teaching Machines." *Cumulative Record*. New York: Appleton-Century-Crofts, 1961. P. 426.

WRITING

In general, all children of four are intensely interested in writing, and some of our children have begun to write at the age of three and a half. We find the children particularly enthusiastic about tracing the sandpaper letters.

—*The Montessori Method*, p. 293

Montessori developed a sequence of indirect and direct preparation for the complex skills involved in writing. The indirect aspects are accomplished largely as "secondary" benefits of sensory education. The child who has worked with the rough and smooth boards, for example, in addition to having exercised the tactile sense, has also gained manual coordination and control which will prove useful in learning to write.

The direct preparation for writing consists of three periods:

1. *Exercises tending to develop the muscular mechanism necessary in (a) holding and (b) using the instrument in writing.*
2. *Exercises tending to establish the visual-muscular image of the alphabet letters, and to establish the "muscular memory" of the movements necessary to writing.*
3. *Exercises for the composition of words.*

Each exercise involves the use of carefully developed didactic material, much of which was prepared by Montessori after "five years' experience of observing the children."

Montessori recognizes the value of a multisensory approach to learning and the importance of the tactile sense in helping the young child grasp reality. The Montessori teacher uses all manner of nonverbal communication, while recognizing the indispensable role that language plays in enabling the child to adapt to life as a rational being. The importance of an optimum environment for full mental and physical development is becoming increasingly clear. Studies made of children from deprived backgrounds indicate that they may suffer irreversible retardation as a result of their lack of normal experiences.

Frank Riessman has termed the formal language deficiencies of culturally deprived children their "Achilles heel." He shifts much of the blame for the poor educational showing of the deprived youngsters from them (and their parents) onto the school which, he maintains, has developed "various forms of subtle, but pervasive, discrimination" against such children.[1] Among the research projects aimed at meeting the experiential needs of deprived city youngsters, the work of Martin Deutsch at the Institute of Developmental Studies has been termed by Charles Silberman "the most important experiment in nursery education for Negro and white slum children."[2] *Many of the techniques being used to encourage various aspects of development are compatible with, if not derived from, the work of Montessori, with which Dr. Deutsch is well acquainted.*

In his article "Schools, Slums, and Montessori," Martin Mayer states that "Montessori was unquestionably correct in her statement that children as young as age four very much want *to read and write, if they get the notion that they* can *read and write."[3] Jerome Bruner advises that "our schools may be wasting precious years by postponing the teaching of many subjects on the grounds that they are too difficult."[4]*

Arthur Jersild suggests that "tremendous potentialities for learning" are being neglected, and proposes an examination of our entire educational program.[5] B. F. Skinner points out that in the lower grades today, "the child is obviously not competent and knows *it," and "the teacher is unable to do anything about it and* knows *that too."[6]*

William Kottmeyer, while superintendent of instruction in a large urban public school system, observed that "poor teaching or poor learning conditions are probably responsible for more reading disability than all the other investigated causes put together."[7] Neurologist Ward Halstead broaches the possibility that our present school situation may be providing a mass medium for impressing neurotic modes of adaptation upon people,[8] while Clifton Fadiman writes that "somehow the average high school graduate does not know who he is, where he is, or how he got there."[9]

Selected References

[1] Riessman, Frank, *The Culturally Deprived Child.* New York: Harper and Row, 1962.

[2] Silberman, Charles, "Give Slum Children a Chance: A Radical Proposal." *Harper's Magazine,* Vol. 228, no. 1368, May, 1964, pp. 39-40.

[3] Mayer, Martin, "Schools, Slums, and Montessori." *Commentary,* Vol. 37, No. 6, June, 1964, p. 37.

[4] Bruner, Jerome, *The Process of Education.* Cambridge, Massachusetts: Harvard University Press, 1960. P. 12.

[5] Jersild, Arthur, "Development as a Product of Learning and Growth." *The Child: A Book of Readings.* Edited by Jerome Seidman. New York: Rinehart. P. 29.

[6] Skinner, B. F., "The Science of Learning and the Art of Teaching." *The Cumulative Record.* New York: Appleton-Century-Crofts, 1961. P. 57.

[7] Kottmeyer, William, *Teacher's Guide for Remedial Action.* St. Louis, Missouri: Webster, 1959. P. 16.

[8] Halstead, Ward, *Brain and Intelligence.* Chicago: University of Chicago Press, 1947. Pp. 141-142.

[9] Fadiman, Clifton, "The Case for Basic Education." *The Case for Basic Education: A Program of Aims for Public Schools.* Boston: Little, Brown, 1959. P. 13.

Writing

Language now comes to *fix* by means of *exact words* the ideas which the mind has acquired. These words are few in number and have reference, not to separate objects, but rather to the *order of the ideas* which have been formed in the mind. In this way the children are able to "find themselves," alike in the world of natural things and in the world of objects and of words which surround them, for they have an inner guide which leads them to become *active and intelligent explorers* instead of wandering wayfarers in an unknown land.

These are the children who, in a short space of time, sometimes in a few days, learn to write and to perform the first operations of arithmetic. It is not a fact that children in general can do it, as many have believed. It is not a case of giving my material for writing to unprepared children and of awaiting the "miracle."

The fact is that the minds and hands of our children are already *prepared* for writing, and ideas of quantity, of identity, of differences, and of gradation, which form the bases of all calculation, have been maturing for a long time in them.

One might say that all their previous education is a preparation for the first stages of essential culture—*writing, reading, and number*; and that knowledge comes as an easy,

spontaneous, and logical consequence of the preparation—
that it is in fact its natural *conclusion*.

We have already seen that the purpose of the *word* is to
fix ideas and to facilitate the elementary comprehension of
things. In the same way writing and arithmetic now fix the
complex inner acquisitions of the mind, which proceeds
henceforward continually to enrich itself by fresh observations.

Our children have long been preparing the hand for
writing. Throughout all the sensory exercises the hand, while
cooperating with the mind in its attainments and in its work
of formation, was preparing its own future. When the hand
learned to hold itself lightly suspended over a horizontal
surface in order to touch rough and smooth, when it took
the cylinders of the solid insets and placed them in their
apertures, when with two fingers it touched the outlines of
the geometrical forms, it was coordinating movements, and
the child is now ready—almost impatient—to use them in the
fascinating "synthesis" of writing.

The *direct* preparation for writing also consists in exercises of the movements of the hand. There are two series
of exercises, very different from one another. I have analyzed
the movements which are connected with writing, and I
prepare them separately one from the other. When we write,
we perform a movement for the *management* of the instrument of writing, a movement which generally acquires an
individual character, so that a person's handwriting can be
recognized, and, in certain medical cases, changes in the
nervous system can be traced by the corresponding altera-
tions in the handwriting. In fact, it is from the handwriting
that specialists in that subject would interpret the *moral
character* of individuals.

Writing has, besides this, a general character, which has
reference to the form of the alphabetical signs.

When a man writes he combines these two parts, but

they actually exist as the *component parts of a single product* and can be prepared apart.

Exercises for the Management of the Instrument of Writing

(THE INDIVIDUAL PART)

In the didactic material there are two sloping wooden boards, on each of which stand five square metal frames, colored pink. In each of these is inserted a blue geometrical figure similar to the geometrical insets and provided with a small button for a handle. With this material we use a box of ten colored pencils and a little book of designs which I have prepared after five years' experience of observing the children. I have chosen and graduated the designs according to the use which the children made of them.

The two sloping boards are set side by side, and on them are placed ten complete "insets," that is to say, the frames with the geometrical figures. The child is given a sheet of white paper and the box of ten colored pencils. He will then choose one of the ten metal insets, which are arranged in an attractive line at a certain distance from him. The child is taught the following process:

He lays the frame of the iron inset on the sheet of paper, and, holding it down firmly with one hand, he follows with a colored pencil the interior outline which describes a geometrical figure. Then he lifts the square frame, and finds drawn upon the paper an enclosed geometrical form, a triangle, a circle, a hexagon, etc. The child has not actually performed a new exercise, because he had already performed all these movements when he *touched* the wooden plane insets. The only new feature of the exercise is that he follows the outlines no longer directly with his finger, but through the medium of a pencil. That is, he *draws, he leaves a trace* of his movement.

The child finds this exercise easy and most interesting,

and, as soon as he has succeeded in making the first outline, he places above it the piece of blue metal corresponding to it. This is an exercise exactly similar to that which he performed when he placed the wooden geometrical figures upon the cards of the third series, where the figures are only contained by a simple line.

This time, however, when the action of placing the form upon the outline is performed, the child takes *another colored pencil* and draws the outline of the blue metal figure.

When he raises it, if the drawing is well done, he finds upon the paper a geometrical figure contained by two outlines in colors, and, if the colors have been well chosen, the result is very attractive, and the child who has already had a considerable education of the chromatic sense, is keenly interested in it.

These may seem unnecessary details, but, as a matter of fact, they are all-important. For instance, if, instead of arranging the ten metal insets in a row, the teacher distributes them among the children without thus exhibiting them, the child's exercises are much limited. When, on the other hand, the insets are exhibited before his eyes, he feels the desire to draw them *all*, one after the other, and the number of exercises is increased.

The two *colored outlines* rouse the desire of the child to see another combination of colors and then to repeat the experience. The variety of the objects and the colors are therefore an *inducement* to work and hence to final success.

Here the actual preparatory movement for writing begins. When the child has drawn the figure in double outline, he takes hold of a pencil "like a pen for writing," and draws marks up and down until he has completely filled the figure. In this way a definite filled-in figure remains on the paper, similar to the figures on the cards of the first series. This figure can be in any of the ten colors. At first the children fill in the figures very clumsily without regard for the outlines, making very heavy lines and not keeping them parallel. Little by little, however, the drawings improve, in that they keep within the outlines, and the lines increase in number, grow finer, and are parallel to one another.

When the child has begun these exercises, he is seized with a desire to continue them, and he never tires of drawing the outlines of the figures and then filling them in. Each child suddenly becomes the possessor of a considerable number of drawings, and he treasures them up in his own little drawer. In this way he *organizes* the movement of writing, which brings him *to the management of the pen.* This movement in ordinary methods is represented by the wearisome pothook connected with the first laborious and tedious attempts at writing.

The organization of this movement, which began from the guidance of a piece of metal, is as yet rough and imperfect, and the child now passes on to the *filling in of the prepared designs* in the little album. The leaves are taken from the book one by one in the order of progression in which they are arranged, and the child fills in the prepared designs with colored pencils in the same way as before. Here the choice of the colors is another intelligent occupation which encourages the child to multiply the tasks. He chooses the colors by himself and with much taste. The delicacy of the shades which he chooses and the harmony with which he arranges them in these designs show us that the common belief, that children love *bright and glaring* colors, has been the result of observation of *children without education,* who have been abandoned to the rough and harsh experiences of an environment unfitted for them.

The education of the chromatic sense becomes at this point of a child's development the *lever* which enables him to become possessed of a firm, bold and beautiful handwriting.

The drawings lend themselves to *limiting,* in very many ways, *the length of the strokes with which they are filled in.*

The child will have to fill in geometrical figures, both large and small, of a pavement design, or flowers and leaves, or the various details of an animal or of a landscape. In this way the hand accustoms itself, not only to perform the general action, but also to confine the movement within all kinds of limits.

Hence the child is preparing himself to write in a handwriting *either* large or small. Indeed, later on he will write as well between the wide lines on a blackboard as between the narrow, closely ruled lines of an exercise book, generally used by much older children.

The number of exercises which the child performs with the drawings is practically unlimited. He will often take another colored pencil and draw over again the outlines of the figure already filled in with color. A help to the *continuation* of the exercise is to be found in the further education of the chromatic sense, which the child acquires by painting the same designs in watercolors. Later he mixes colors for himself until he can imitate the colors of nature, or create the delicate tints which his own imagination desires. It is not possible, however, to speak of all this in detail within the limits of this small work.

Exercises for the Writing of Alphabetical Signs

In the didactic material there are series of boxes which contain the alphabetical signs. At this point we take those cards which are covered with very smooth paper, to which is gummed a letter of the alphabet cut out in sandpaper. There are also large cards on which are gummed several letters, grouped together according to analogy of form.

The children "have to *touch* over the alphabetical signs as though they were writing." They touch them with the tips of the index and middle fingers in the same way as when they touched the wooden insets, and with the hand raised as when they lightly touched the rough and smooth surfaces.

The teacher herself touches the letters to show the child how the movement should be performed, and the child, if he has had much practice in touching the wooden insets, *imitates* her with *ease* and pleasure. Without the previous practice, however, the child's hand does not follow the letter with accuracy, and it is most interesting to make close observations of the children in order to understand the importance of a *remote motor preparation* for writing, and also to realize the *immense* strain which we impose upon the children when we set them to write directly without a previous motor education of the hand.

The child finds great pleasure in touching the sandpaper letters. It is an exercise by which he applies to a new attainment the power he has already acquired through exercising the sense of touch. While the child touches a letter, the teacher pronounces its sound, and she uses for the lesson the usual three periods. Thus, for example, presenting the two vowels *i, o,* she will have the child touch them slowly and accurately, and repeat their relative sounds one after the other as the child touches them, "i, i, i! o, o, o!" Then she will say to the child: "Give me i!" "Give me o!" Finally, she will ask the question: "What is this?" To which the child replies, "i, o." She proceeds in the same way through all the other letters, giving, in the case of the consonants, not the name, but only the sound. The child then touches the letters by himself over and over again, either on the separate cards or on the large cards on which several letters are gummed, and in this way he establishes the movements necessary for tracing the alphabetical signs. At the same time he retains the *visual* image of the letter. This process forms the first preparation, not only for writing, but also for reading, because it is evident that when the child *touches* the letters he performs the movement corresponding to the writing of them, and, at the same time, when he recognizes them by sight he is reading the alphabet.

The child has thus prepared, in effect, all the necessary

movements for writing; therefore he *can write*. This important conquest is the result of a long period of inner formation of which the child is not clearly aware. But a day will come—very soon—when he *will write*, and that will be a day of great surprise for him—the wonderful harvest of an unknown sowing.

The alphabet of movable letters cut out in pink and blue cardboard, and kept in a special box with compartments, serves "for the composition of words."

In a phonetic language, like Italian, it is enough to pronounce clearly the different component sounds of a word (as, for example, m-a-n-o), so that the child whose ear is *already educated* may recognize one by one the component sounds. Then he looks in the movable alphabet for the *signs* corresponding to each separate sound, and lays them one beside the other, thus composing the word (for instance, mano). Gradually he will become able to do the same thing with words of which he thinks himself; he succeeds in breaking them up into their component sounds, and in translating them into a row of signs.

When the child has composed the words in this way, he knows how to read them. In this method, therefore, all the processes leading to writing include reading as well.

If the language is not phonetic, the teacher can compose separate words with the movable alphabet, and then pronounce them, letting the child repeat by himself the exercise of arranging and rereading them.

In the material there are two movable alphabets. One of them consists of larger letters, and is divided into two boxes, each of which contains the vowels. This is used for the first exercises, in which the child needs very large objects in order to recognize the letter. When he is acquainted with one half of the consonants he can begin "to compose words, even though he is dealing with one part only of the alphabet.

The other movable alphabet has smaller letters and is

contained in a single box. It is given to children who have made their first attempts at composition with words, and already know the complete alphabet.

It is after these exercises with the movable alphabet that the child *is able to write entire words*. This phenomenon generally occurs unexpectedly, and then a child who has never yet traced a stroke or a letter on paper *writes several words in succession*. From that moment he continues to write, always gradually perfecting himself. This spontaneous writing takes on the characteristics of a *natural* phenomenon, and the child who has begun to write the "first word" will continue to write in the same way as he spoke after pronouncing the first word, and as he walked after having taken the first step. The same course of inner formation through which the phenomenon of writing appeared is the course of his future progress, of his growth to perfection. The child prepared in this way has entered upon a course of development through which he will pass as surely as the growth of the body and the development of the natural functions have passed through their course of development when life has once been established.

For the interesting and very complex phenomena relating to the development of writing and then of reading, see my larger works.

ARITHMETIC

Not only is it possible to perform long division with our bead material, but the work is so delightful that it becomes an arithmetical pastime especially adapted to the child's home activities.

—*The Montessori Elementary Materials*, p. 237

Although we find Arnold and Beatrice Gesell admitting in 1912, the year The Montessori Method *first appeared in*

English translation, that "the Montessori arithmetical apparatus has many excellent uses,"[1] there has been no concerted effort in America to study the readiness of the young child for learning mathematics. Thomas Balliet, dean of the School of Pedagogy of New York University, for example, wrote in the 1916 National Education Association Addresses and Proceedings that children "will know just as much arithmetic at the end of the fifth year of school if it be begun in the fourth year as they will if it be begun in the first."[2] Such a statement is representative of what could be termed the "cult of readiness" approach to early childhood education which has held sway for half a century in this country. But, as Jerome Bruner notes in his essay "On Learning Mathematics," readiness "is a function not so much of maturation as it is of our intentions and our skill at translating ideas into the language and concepts of the age level we are teaching."[3]

Montessori speaks of the "mathematical mind" of the child—that part of the mind "which is built up with exactitude" and reflects a natural mathematical tendency in the young child toward precision, classification and measurement. The child, bent on bringing form and order into his environment, constructs from experience internal "models" or "maps" of that environment which serve in the future as bases upon which to make decisions. This "need to qualify," to abstract and internalize environmental consistencies, may not be met in an inconsistent or impoverished setting, where the child is not furnished the necessary means and materials. A disorderly environment will likely result in a disorderly mind.

Work with the Montessori mathematical material may be said to give a child an alphabet for the language of mathematics. The Montessori child, provided the freedom and means to engage and master the "prepared environment" during his "preschool" years is indeed ready by age six for a "new kind of school for the acquisition of culture."

In an early critique of the Montessori method, the Gesells indicate our schools do not need "devices, technical apparatus and systematized processes" inasmuch as "such order and progression" is not found in the child's learning process. According to the Gesells, most children have enough opportunity in their daily activities to handle and touch various forms and surfaces.[4] But, as B. F. Skinner has recognized, the contingencies of reinforcement responsible for human discriminative learning are "quite rare in the environment of the average child." Although children may be encouraged to play with objects of various sizes, shapes, and colors, they are "seldom exposed to the precise contingencies needed to build subtle discriminations."[5]

Selected References

[1] Gesell, Arnold and Beatrice, *The Normal Child and Primary Education.* Boston: Ginn, 1912. P. 337.

[2] Balliet, Thomas, "Practical Means of Unifying the Work of the Kindergarten and the Primary Grades." *National Education Association Address and Proceedings,* Vol. LIV, 1916. P. 438.

[3] Bruner, Jerome, "On Learning Mathematics." In *On Knowing: Essays for the Left Hand.* Cambridge, Massachusetts: The Belknap Press of Harvard University Press, 1962. P. 108.

[4] Gesell, Arnold and Beatrice, *The Normal Child and Primary Education.* Boston: Ginn, 1912. Pp. 335-336.

[5] Skinner, B. F., "Why We Need Teaching Machines." *Cumulative Record.* New York: Appleton-Century-Crofts, 1961. Pp. 182-205.

Arithmetic

The children possess all the instinctive knowledge necessary as a preparation for clear ideas on numeration. The idea of quantity was inherent in all the material for the education of the senses: longer, shorter, darker, lighter. The conception of identity and of difference formed part of the actual technique of the education of the senses, which began with the recognition of identical objects, and continued with the arrangements in gradation of similar objects. I will make a special illustration of the first exercise with the solid insets, which can be done even by a child of two and a half. When he makes a mistake by putting a cylinder in a hole too large for it, and so leaves *one* cylinder without a place, he instinctively absorbs the idea of the absence of *one* from a continuous series. The child's mind is not prepared for number "by certain preliminary ideas," given in haste by the teacher, but has been prepared for it by a process of formation, by a slow building up of itself.

To enter directly upon the teaching of arithmetic, we must turn to the same didactic material used for the education of the senses.

Let us look at the three sets of material which are presented after the exercises with the solid insets, *i.e.*, the material for teaching *size* (the pink cubes), *thickness* (the brown prisms), and *length* (the green rods). There is a definite relation between the ten pieces of each series. In the material for length the shortest piece is a *unit of measurement* for all the rest; the second piece is double the first, the third is three times the first, etc., and while the scale of length increases by ten centimeters for each piece, the other dimensions remain constant (*i.e.*, the rods all have the same section).

The pieces then stand in the same relation to one another as the natural series of the numbers 1, 2, 3, 4, 5, 6, 7, 8, 9, 10.

In the second series, namely, that which shows *thickness*, while the length remains constant, the square section of the prisms varies. The result is that the sides of the square sections vary according to the series of natural numbers; *i.e.*, in the first prism, the square of the section has sides of one ˜˜ntimeter, in the second of two centimeters, in the third of three centimeters, etc., and so on until the tenth, in which the square of the section has sides of ten centimeters. The prisms therefore are in the same proportion to one another as the numbers of the series of squares (1, 4, 9, etc.), for it would take four prisms of the first size to make the second, nine to make the third, etc. The pieces which make up the series for teaching thickness are therefore in the following proportion: 1 : 4 : 9 : 16 : 25 : 36 : 49 : 64 : 81 : 100.

In the case of the pink cubes the edge increases according to the numerical series; *i.e.*, the first cube has an edge of one centimeter, the second of two centimeters, the third of three centimeters, and so on, to the tenth cube, which has an edge of ten centimeters. Hence the relation in volume between them is that of the cubes of the series of numbers from one to ten; *i.e.*, 1 : 8 : 27 : 64 : 125 : 216 : 343 : 512 : 729 : 1,000. In fact, to make up the volume of the second pink cube, eight of the first little cubes would be required; to make up the volume of the third, twenty-seven would be required, and so on.

The children have an intuitive knowledge of this difference, for they realize that the exercise with the pink cubes is the *easiest* of all three and that with the rods the most difficult. When we begin the direct teaching of number, we choose the long rods, modifying them, however, by dividing them into ten spaces, each ten centimeters in length, colored alternately red and blue. For example, the rod which is four times as long as the first is clearly seen to be composed of four equal lengths, red and blue; and similarly with all the rest.

When the rods have been placed in order of gradation, we teach the child the numbers: one, two, three, etc., by touching the rods in succession, from the first up to ten. Then, to help him to gain a clear idea of number, we proceed to the recognition of separate rods by means of the customary lesson in three periods.

We lay the three first rods in front of the child, and pointing to them or taking them in the hand in turn, in order to show them to him, we say: "This is *one*." "This is *two*." "This is *three*." We point out with the finger the divisions in each rod, counting them so as to make sure, "One, two: this is *two*." "One, two, three: this is *three*." Then we say

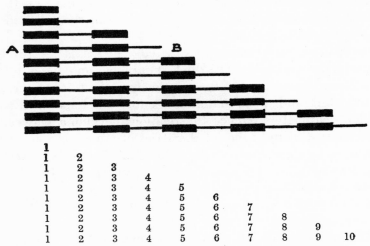

1									
1	2								
1	2	3							
1	2	3	4						
1	2	3	4	5					
1	2	3	4	5	6				
1	2	3	4	5	6	7			
1	2	3	4	5	6	7	8		
1	2	3	4	5	6	7	8	9	
1	2	3	4	5	6	7	8	9	10

DIAGRAM ILLUSTRATING USE OF NUMERICAL RODS.

to the child: "Give me *two*." "Give me *one*." "Give me *three*." Finally, pointing to a rod, we say, "What is this?" The child answers, "Three," and we count together: "One, two, three."

In the same way we teach all the other rods in their order, adding always one or two more according to the responsiveness of the child.

The importance of this didactic material is that it gives a clear idea of *number*. For when a number is named it exists as an object, a unity in itself. When we say that a man possesses a million, we mean that he has a *fortune* which is worth so many units of measure of values, and these units all belong to one person.

So, if we add 7 to 8 (7 + 8), we add a *number to a number*, and these numbers for a *definite* reason represent in themselves groups of homogeneous units.

Again, when the child shows us the 9, he is handling a rod which is inflexible—an object complete in itself, yet composed of *nine equal parts* which can be counted. And when he comes to add 8 to 2, he will place next to one another two rods, two objects, one of which has eight equal lengths and the other two. When, on the other hand, in ordinary schools, to make the calculation easier, they present the child with different objects to count, such as beans, marbles, etc., and when, to take the case I have quoted $(8 + 2)$, he takes a group of eight marbles and adds two more marbles to it, the natural impression in his mind is not that he has added 8 to 2, but that he has added $1 + 1 + 1 + 1 + 1 + 1 + 1 + 1$ to $1 + 1$. The result is not so clear, and the child is required to make the effort of holding in his mind the idea of a group of eight objects as *one united whole*, corresponding to a single number, 8.

This effort often puts the child back, and delays his understanding of number by months or even years.

The addition and subtraction of numbers under ten are made very much simpler by the use of the didactic material for teaching lengths. Let the child be presented with the attractive problem of arranging the pieces in such a way as to have a set of rods, all as long as the longest. He first arranges the rods in their right order (the long stair); he then takes the last rod (1) and lays it next to the 9. Similarly, he takes the last rod but one (2) and lays it next to the 8, and so on up to the 5.

This very simple game represents the addition of numbers within the ten: $9 + 1$, $8 + 2$, $7 + 3$, $6 + 4$. Then, when he puts the rods back in their places, he must first take away the 4 and put it back under the 5, and then take away in their turn the 3, the 2, the 1. By this action he has put the rods back again in their right gradation, but he has also performed a series of arithmetical subtractions, $10 - 4$, $10 - 3$, $10 - 2$, $10 - 1$.

The teaching of the actual figures marks an advance from the rods to the process of counting with separate units. When the figures are known, they will serve the very purpose in the abstract which the rods serve in the concrete; that is, they will stand for the *uniting into one whole* of a certain number of separate units.

The *synthetic* function of language and the wide field of work which it opens out for the intelligence is *demonstrated*, we might say, by the function of the *figure*, which now can be substituted for the concrete rods.

The use of the actual rods only would limit arithmetic to the small operations within the ten or numbers a little higher, and, in the construction of the mind, these operations would advance very little farther than the limits of the first simple and elementary education of the senses.

The figure, which is a word, a graphic sign, will permit of that unlimited progress which the mathematical mind of man has been able to make in the course of its evolution.

In the material there is a box containing smooth cards, on which are gummed the figures from one to nine, cut out in sandpaper. These are analogous to the cards on which are gummed the sandpaper letters of the alphabet. The method of teaching is always the same. The child is *made to touch* the figures in the direction in which they are written, and to name them at the same time.

In this case he does more than when he learned the letters; he is shown how to place each figure upon the corresponding rod. When all the figures have been learned in this way, one of the first exercises will be to place the number cards upon the rods arranged in gradation. So arranged, they form a succession of steps on which it is a pleasure to place the cards, and the children remain for a long time repeating this intelligent game.

After this exercise comes what we may call the "emancipation" of the child. He carried his own figures with him, and now *using them* he will know how to group units together.

For this purpose we have in the didactic material a series of wooden pegs, but in addition to these we give the children all sorts of small objects—sticks, tiny cubes, counters, etc.

The exercise will consist in placing opposite a figure the number of objects that it indicates. The child for this purpose can use the box which is included in the material. This box is divided into compartments, above each of which is printed a figure, and the child places in the compartment the corresponding number of pegs.

Another exercise is to lay all the figures on the table and place below them the corresponding number of cubes, counters, etc.

This is only the first step, and it would be impossible here to speak of the succeeding lessons in zero, in tens and in other arithmetical processes—for the development of which my larger works must be consulted. The didactic material itself, however, can give some idea. In the box containing the pegs there is one compartment over which the 0 is printed. Inside this compartment "nothing must be put," and then we begin with *one*.

Zero is nothing, but it is placed next to one to enable us to count when we pass beyond 9—thus, 10.

If, instead of the piece 1, we were to take pieces as long as the rod 10, we could count 10, 20, 30, 40, 50, 60, 70, 80, 90. In the didactic material there are frames containing cards on which are printed such numbers from 10 to 90. These numbers are fixed into a frame in such a way that the figures 1 to 9 can be slipped in covering the zero. If the zero of 10 is covered by 1 the result is 11, if with 2 it becomes 12, and so on, until the last 9. Then we pass to the twenties (the second ten), and so on, from ten to ten.

For the beginning of this exercise with the cards marking the tens we can use the rods. As we begin with the first ten (10) in the frame, we take the rod 10. We then place the small rod 1 next to rod 10, and at the same time slip in the number 1, covering the zero of the 10. Then we take rod 1 and figure 1 away from the frame, and put in their place rod 2 next to rod 10, and figure 2 over the zero in the frame, and so on, up to 9. To advance farther we should need to use two rods of 10 to make 20.

The children show much enthusiasm when learning these exercises, which demand from them two sets of activities, and give them in their work clearness of idea.

In writing and arithmetic we have gathered the fruits of a laborious education which consisted in coordinating the movements and gaining a first knowledge of the world. This culture comes as a natural consequence of man's first efforts to put himself into intelligent communication with the world.

All those early acquisitions which have brought order into the child's mind would be wasted were they not firmly established by means of written language and of figures. Thus established, however, these experiences open up an unlimited field for future education. What we have done, therefore, is to introduce the child to a higher level—the level of culture—and he will now be able to pass on to a *school*, but not the school we know today, where, irrationally, we try to give culture to minds not yet prepared or *educated to receive it*.

To preserve the health of their minds, which have been *exercised* and not *fatigued* by the order of the work, our children must have a new kind of school for the acquisition of culture. My experiments in the continuation of this method for older children are already far advanced.

V

A NEW CHILD—A NEW MAN

Instead of giving out what she has in herself, the teacher must bring out the full possibilities of the children.

—*The Montessori Elementary Materials*, p. 44

Montessori and the World of Work

IN the more than half century that has elapsed since Dr. Maria Montessori began making her remarkable contributions to the philosophy and methodology of education there has been developing in American educational practice a cleavage that can be observed in almost any American city. We have, on the one hand, the fruits of long years of effort to implement the principles so well expressed and exemplified by Dr. Montessori and other educational innovators. We find, in many of our more favored metropolitan educational institutions, the will and the means to provide children and youth with controlled situations in which they can respond to the challenges of progressively more demanding tasks, through which their sensitivities, understandings, skills —and most of all their values and goals—can be developed. On the other hand, in the decaying "inner city" of many urban centers, and in the nation's outlying depressed areas, there are vast and growing numbers of children and youth whose life experiences at home, on the street and in the school are, on the whole, stultifying if not degrading and almost totally lacking in the kinds of challenge that could develop their potentials for personal growth and achievement.

Most of us are familiar with the stereotype of the slum school. In the depressed rural area it is a forlorn relic of the nineteenth century. In the city it occupies a barnlike, obsolete structure with defective plumbing, lighting, ventilation and heating. It is devoid of shops, libraries or other special facilities. It is surrounded by a sun-baked yard into which the children are herded at recess time. The classrooms are

153

crowded, the children regimented in solid rows, at desks screwed to the floor. The textbooks are outdated. The teacher, with far too many pupils, is forced to abandon her proper role as mentor and guide.

Unlike the Montessori teacher, who functions as a "perceiver" of the child's needs, a "preparer" of his environment, and a "provider" of a living example of what the child may become, the "slum teacher" must often instead be a pacesetter for the group as a whole, dispensing information regardless of the readiness or interest of the individual child. A substantial part of her task is to keep some semblance of order. She does what she can to command attention, and uses tests, recitations and other devices to check upon what the children may have absorbed and can report back verbally. A tiny, overworked staff of special teachers spread themselves thinly over the many children who need remedial reading instruction, correction of speech defects and other special attention.

What can we do to alleviate this situation? For one thing, we can recognize, with Dr. Montessori, that these culturally deprived or disadvantaged youths have within themselves, in spite of the treatment they have received thus far in their lives, a basic capacity for sustained and serious effort—in other words, for learning and work.

But this capacity must be developed by giving them the opportunity to achieve sequences of success in school and on the job. We must bring them into close relations with situations in which it will be clear to them that what they learn will have some tangible value and utility. We can no longer vainly hope, for example, that dropouts will go back to school and pick up where they left off in subjects that have no bearing on their present lives or immediate vocational futures. Telling them in the abstract about the importance—even the statistics of the dollar value—of education is futile. The new programs, properly planned, must make learning flow out of work—work of a type and in a setting that teaches its own lessons. This is very possible and practical, whether it is carried on through job training in conservation work in a youth camp, in some local community development project, in a repair or service shop course in a school, or in on-the-job training with a prospective employer.

These programs need to be presented with a structured framework. Deprived youngsters are insecure and are constantly testing the limits of their environment. A structured environment is not a rigid environment but a framework that provides security and reduces the threat of the unknown. This insecurity is related to the lack of self-discipline that is so common in the culture of the disadvantaged. Consistency must also prevail in the experiences that we expose these youngsters to. For a major portion of their lives they have been unable to depend on anything other than failure, rejection and frustration. They are a product of their culture, and as a result what we are actually trying to do is change a way of life that has been handed down from generation to generation. Trying to change the value system of a human being is a major undertaking. These youngsters, of course, have a code of the values just as we do. But these values are not the same as the ones we hold in our middle-class culture.

To ever really get to the heart of this problem, we must start with the youngsters at a very early age instead of waiting until they are teen-agers. New programs must be developed at the preprimary level that will take the child from a sordid home situation and present him with experiences that will help insulate him against the frustrations and anxieties rampant in slum surroundings, while, of course, we must work to eliminate these unhygienic environments.

Such programs must provide the success that will nurture his self-concept; they must provide structure and security allowing him to develop self-discipline; they must provide opportunities that will cultivate his curiosity and interest; they must provide for a sense of privacy and possession so lacking in his own home. To staff programs of this type we need sensitive competent teachers who, by virtue of their spirit and skill, could fairly be described by the term "Montessorian." And ultimately, of course, our educational reforms for the deprived child must be matched by a rebuilding of his physical world.

WILLIAM E. AMOS, ED.D.

DISCIPLINE IN REVIEW

The spontaneous discipline, and the obedience which is manifested throughout the whole class, constitute the most striking result of our method.

—*Dr. Montessori's Own Handbook*, p. 130 (original)

Alfred North Whitehead, who refers to the "success of the Montessori system," writes that "in no part of education can you do without discipline or can you do without freedom."[1] William Heard Kilpatrick wrote in 1914 that the Montessori system "accords a remarkable degree of freedom to the individual children. . . ." He indicated further that "we highly approve Madam Montessori's reemphasis of the doctrine of liberty. In the practical outworking of her idea she has set an example to home, to kindergarten, and to primary school." In summing up her contribution he says:

> *Her greatest service lies probably in the emphasis on the scientific conception of education, and the practical utilization of liberty.[2]*

The Montessori Method may be conceived as a systematic removing of obstacles to the child's development, the most formidable obstacles being unenlightened adults. Most children are mentally malnourished; they need and want work —that is, experience in mastering interesting tasks. Children also require the security derived from sufficient structure in their environment.

In starting a new class, the Montessori directress establishes certain definite limits or "ground rules," which are simple and few in number but are consistently maintained, freeing the child to be independent and to exercise mobility. For example, a child may not touch another child's work, unless invited to by that child. This is important because, to the young child, his work is an extension of himself—his ego. Work and worker are the same.

The child works on his own little carpet, or at his own "sacred space" on a table, knowing that his work will be respected by everyone else. If he has to leave the room for any reason he can do so secure in the knowledge that when he returns he will find his activity in the same condition in which he left it. This rule makes possible a great deal of mobility in the learning situation, where all children are doing different things under the direction of one or perhaps two teachers.

Montessori' writings, like those of Jerome Bruner, agree with Whitehead's belief that "from the very beginning of his education, the child should experience the joy of discovery." Bruner says, "Discovery, like surprise favors the well-prepared mind";[3] and Montessori has written, "It matters much more to have a prepared mind than to have a good teacher."[4] For Whitehead, there can be no mental development without interest. The mind, never passive, is a "perpetual activity, delicate, receptive, responsive to stimulus." The environment within which the mind is working must be carefully selected to suit the child's stage of growth and adapted to his individual needs. "In a sense it is an imposition from without," says Whitehead, "but in a deeper sense it answers to the call of life within the child."[5] The purpose of education is to stimulate and guide self-development; the one subject matter of education is "life in all its manifestations."[6]

Alexandra Adler, daughter of Alfred Adler, the founder of "individual psychology," emphasizes repeatedly in her book, Guiding Human Misfits, that the early formative childhood years set the pattern for later life. She notes that in all genuises one can trace "intensive early training," and refers to the role of Nancy Elliott Edison, mother of the great American inventor, in instructing her son Thomas. According to Alexandra Adler, the intuitions of a genius are the result of long, arduous training; his ideas always pertaining to "his special field of work."[7]

Francis Galton, many years ago, wrote, "It is, I believe, owing to the favourable conditions of their early training, that an unusually large proportion of the sons of the most gifted men of science become distinguished in the same career."[8] E. M. Standing, in a study of Montessori, tells that soon after her arrival in America, Montessori became a guest of the family of Edison, "who had a great admiration for her work,"[9] and she herself referred to Edison as "one of the first friends of the Montessori Method."[10]

Selected References

[1] Whitehead, Alfred North, *The Aims of Education and Other Essays.* New York: New American Library, 1951. P. 41.

[2] Kilpatrick, William Heard, *The Montessori System Examined.* Boston: Houghton Mifflin, 1914. P. 67.

[3] Bruner, Jerome, "The Act of Discovery." *On Knowing: Essays for the Left Hand.* Cambridge, Massachusetts: Belnap Press of Harvard University Press, 1962. P. 82.

[4] Montessori, Maria, *The Absorbent Mind.* Adyar, Madras 20, India: The Theosophical Publishing House, Third Edition, 1961. P. 183.

[5] Whitehead, Alfred North, *The Aims of Education and Other Essays.* New York: New American Library, 1949. Pp. 42ff.

[6] *Ibid.*, p. 18.

[7] Adler, Alexandra, *Guiding Human Misfits.* London: Faber and Faber, Second Edition, 1948. Pp. 24 f.

[8] Galton, Francis, *Hereditary Genius: An Inquiry into Its Laws and Consequences.* London: Macmillan, 1892. Pp. 189-190.

[9] Standing, E. M., *Maria Montessori: Her Life and Work.* Fresno, California: Academy Library Guild, 1959. P. 44.

[10] Montessori, Maria, *To Educate the Human Potential.* Adyar, Madras 20, India: Kalakshetia Publications, 1956. P. 123.

Discipline in Review

A brief description such as this, of the *means* which are used in the "Children's House," may perhaps give the reader the impression of a logical and convincing system of education. But the importance of my method does not lie in the organization itself, but *in the effects which it produces on the child*. It is the *child* who proves the value of this method by his spontaneous manifestations, which seem to reveal the laws of man's inner development. Psychology will perhaps find in the "Children's Houses" a laboratory which will bring more truths to light than thus hitherto recognized; for the essential factor in psychological research, especially in the field of psychogenesis, the origin and development of the mind, must be the establishment of normal conditions for the free development of thought.

As is well known, we leave the children *free* in their work, and in all actions which are not of a disturbing kind. That is, we *eliminate* disorder, which is "bad," but allow to that which is orderly and "good" the most complete liberty of manifestation.

The results obtained are surprising, for the children have shown a love of work which no one suspected to be in them, and a calm and an orderliness in their movements which, surpassing the limit of correctness, have entered into those of "grace." The spontaneous discipline, and the obedience which is seen in the whole class, constitute the most striking result of our method.

The ancient philosophical discussion as to whether man is born good or evil is often brought forward in connection with my method, and many who have supported it have done so on the ground that it provides a demonstration of man's natural goodness. Very many others, on the contrary, have opposed it, considering that to leave children free is a dangerous mistake, since they have in them innate tendencies to evil.

I should like to put the question upon a more positive plane.

In the words "good" and "evil" we include the most varying ideas, and we confuse them especially *in our practical dealings with little children.*

The tendencies which we stigmatize as *evil* in little children of three to six years of age are often merely those which cause *annoyance* to us adults when, not understanding their needs, we try to prevent their *every movement,* their every *attempt to gain experience for themselves in the world* (by touching everything, etc.). The child, however, through this *natural tendency,* is led to *coordinate his movements* and to collect impressions, especially sensations of touch, so that when prevented he *rebels,* and this rebellion forms almost the whole of his "naughtiness."

What wonder is it that the evil disappears when, if we give the right *means* for development and leave full liberty to use them, rebellion has no more reason for existence?

Further, by the substitution of a series of outbursts of *joy* for the old series of outbursts of *rage,* the "moral physiognomy" of the child comes to assume a calm and gentleness which make him appear a different being.

It is we who provoked the children to the violent manifestations of a real *struggle for existence.* In order to exist *according to the needs of their psychic development* they were often obliged to snatch from us the things which seemed necessary to them for the purpose. They had to move contrary to our laws, or sometimes to struggle with other children to wrest from them the objects of their desire.

On the other hand, if we give children the *means of existence,* the struggle for it disappears, and a vigorous expansion of life takes its place. This question involves a hygienic principle connected with the nervous system during the difficult period when the brain is still rapidly growing, and should be of great interest to specialists in children's diseases and nervous derangements. The inner life of man and the beginnings of his intellect are controlled by special laws and vital necessities which cannot be forgotten if we are aiming at health for mankind.

For this reason, an educational method which cultivates and protects the inner activities of the child is not a question which concerns merely the school or the teachers; it is a universal question which concerns the family, and is of vital interest to mothers.

To go more deeply into a question is often the only means of answering it rightly. If, for instance, we were to see men fighting over a piece of bread, we might say: "How bad men are!" If, on the other hand, we entered a well-warmed eating house, and saw them quietly finding a place and choosing their meal without any envy of one another, we might say: "How good men are!" Evidently, the question of absolute good and evil, intuitive ideas of which guide us in our superficial judgment, goes beyond such limitations as these. We can, for instance, provide excellent eating houses for an entire people without directly affecting the question of their morals. One might say, indeed, that to judge by appearances, a well-fed people are *better, quieter, and commit less crime* than a nation that is ill-nourished; but whoever draws from that the conclusion to make men good it is *enough* to feed them, will be making an obvious mistake.

It cannot be denied, however, that *nourishment* will be an essential factor in obtaining goodness, in the sense that it will *eliminate* all the *evil acts, and the bitterness* caused by lack of bread.

Now, in our case, we are dealing with a far deeper need— the nourishment of man's inner life, and of his higher functions. The bread that we are dealing with is the bread of the spirit, and we are entering into the difficult subject of the satisfaction of man's psychic needs.

We have already obtained a most interesting result, in that we have found it possible to present *new means* of enabling children to reach a higher level of calm and goodness, and we have been able to establish these means by experience. The whole foundation of our results rests upon these means which we have discovered, and which may be divided under two heads—the *organization of work,* and liberty.

It is the perfect organization of work, permitting the possibility of self-development and giving outlet for the energies, which procures for each child the beneficial and calming *satisfaction.* And it is under such conditions of work that liberty leads to a perfecting of the activities, and to the attainment of a fine discipline which is in itself the result of that new quality of *calmness* that has been developed in the child.

Freedom without organization of work would be useless. The child left *free* without means of work would go to waste, just as a newborn baby, if *left free* without nourishment, would die of starvation. *The organization of the work,* therefore, is the cornerstone of this new structure of goodness; but even that organization would be in vain without the *liberty* to make use of it, and without freedom for the expansion of all those energies which spring from the satisfaction of the child's highest activities.

Has not a similar phenomenon occurred also in the history of man? The history of civilization is a history of successful attempts to organize work and to obtain liberty. On the whole, man's goodness has also increased, as is shown by his progress from barbarism to civilization, and it may be said that crime, the various forms of wickedness, cruelty and violence have been gradually decreasing during this passage of time.

The *criminality* of our times, as a matter of fact, has been compared to a form of *barbarism* surviving in the midst of civilized peoples. It is, therefore, through the better organization of work that society will probably attain to a further purification, and in the meanwhile it seems unconsciously to be seeking the overthrow of the last barriers between itself and liberty.

If this is what we learn from society, how great should be the results among little children from three to six years of age if the organization of their work is complete, and their freedom absolute? It is for this reason that to us they seem so good, like heralds of hope and of redemption.

If men, walking as yet so painfully and imperfectly along the road of work and of freedom, have become better, why should we fear that the same road will prove disastrous to the children?

Yet, on the other hand, I would not say that the goodness of our little ones in their freedom will solve the problem of the absolute goodness or wickedness of man. We can only say that we have made a contribution to the cause of goodness by removing obstacles which were the cause of violence and of rebellion.

Let us "render, therefore, unto Caesar the things that are Caesar's, and unto God the things that are God's."

THE NEW EDUCATION

It is the children themselves who spread my method. Happily they behave as I say they do in my books, and people go and see them, and at last believe it themselves.

—*The Child in the Church*, p. 184

Montessori began a later book, The Secret of Childhood, *with a discussion of the topic "The Century of the Child," which is also the title of a celebrated book by Swedish author Ellen Keys. Montessori believed that the twentieth century would mark a new and glorious era (begun during the last decade of the nineteenth century) for realization of the child's rights, and the resolution of the "social question of the child," the "question of our present and our future." For a whole chapter covering in detail the points only touched upon in this section, the reader should consult "A Survey of the Child's Life," Chapter One in Montessori's* Spontaneous Activity in Education *(Volume One of* The Advanced Montessori Method), *where she mentions that historically statistics of infant mortality "reveal figures so high that the phenomenon may justly be called the 'Slaughter of the Innocents.' "*

Related to the idea of the emergence of a new race is Montessori's notion of the "medial man." This term refers to the prototype of the new race, to be ideally proportioned and perfectly developed morphologically, intellectually and morally. Montessori discusses this subject at length in Chapter Ten, "The Application of Biometry to Anthropology for the Purpose of Determining the Medial Man," in her book Pedagogical Anthropology *(New York: Frederick Stokes, 1913), and refers especially to the work of Quetelet and Viola.*

Montessori has written, "The teacher must consecrate herself to the formation of a better humanity."[1] The most important task of adults, then, is facilitating the child's inner work by safeguarding his natural development. Science has evolved a physical hygiene; now, a scientific pedagogy is needed to discover and implement the condition fostering mental health and the "expansion of the intellect."

Other physical and social scientists have been voicing similar hopes in recent years. Anthropologist William Howells notes that we "have only begun to explore the larger possibilities of brains since we left the caves."[2] Biologist Julian Huxley tells us that man's destiny is "to participate and lead in the creative process of evolution, whereby new possibilities can be realized for life."[3] B. F. Skinner in his article "Why We Need Teaching Machines" has given the goal of education as "nothing short of the fullest possible development of the human organism."[4] Now, according to L. K. Frank, we have "a truly inspiring conception of man as an organism with hitherto unrecognized potentialities." Man has, in short, a new image of himself.[5]

Montessori describes in The Montessori Method *the "new children" that the prepared environment of the "Children's House" revealed. "These children pronounce clearly, write in a firm hand, and are full of grace in their movements. They are the earnest [pledge] of a humanity grown in the cult of beauty—the infancy of an all-conquering humanity, since they are intelligent and patient observers of their environment, and possess in the form of intellectual liberty the power of spontaneous reasoning."[6]*

Francis Galton's study of his own mental imagery and that of others testifies to the effect of individual differences in experience, and to the permanence of many results of early education. As part of his researches, he queried other persons concerning their thought processes. The following quotation is from his Inquiries Into Human Faculty and Its Development:

> *Thus one correspondent, of no mean literary and philosophical power, recollects the left hand by a mental reference to the rocking-horse which always stood by the side of the nursery wall with its head in the same direction, and had to be mounted from the side next the wall. Another, a politician, historian, and scholar, refers all his dates to the mental image of a nursery diagram of the history of the world, which has since developed huge bosses to support his later acquired information.[7]*

Selected References

[1] Montessori, Maria, *The Child*. Adyar, Madras 20, India: Theosophical Publishing House, 1961. P. 26.

[2] Howells, William, *Mankind So Far*. Garden City, New York: Doubleday, 1950. Pp. 308-309.

[3] Huxley, Julian, *Evolution in Action*. London: Chatto and Windus, 1953. P. 133.

[4] Skinner, B. F., "Why We Need Teaching Machines." *Cumulative Record*. New York: Appleton-Century-Crofts, 1961. P. 182.

[5] Frank, Lawrence K., *Nature and Human Nature*. New Brunswick, New Jersey: Rutgers University Press, 1951. P. 152.

[6] Montessori, Maria, *The Montessori Method*. New York, Frederick Stokes, 1912.

[7] Galton, Francis, *Inquiries Into Human Faculty and Its Development*. London: J. M. Dent, Second Edition, 1907. Pp. 131-132.

The New Education

Recent years have seen a remarkable improvement in the conditions of child life. In all civilized countries, statistics show a decrease in infant mortality.

Related to this decrease in mortality a corresponding improvement is to be seen in the physical development of children; they are physically finer and more vigorous. It has been the diffusion, the popularization of science, which has brought about such notable advantages. Mothers have learned to welcome the dictates of modern hygiene and to put them into practice in bringing up their children. Many new social institutions have sprung up and have been perfected with the object of assisting children and protecting them during the period of physical growth.

In this way, what is practically a new race is coming into being, a race more highly developed, finer and more robust; a race which will be capable of offering resistance to insidious disease.

What has science done to effect this? Science has suggested for us certain very simple rules by which the child has been restored as nearly as possible to conditions of a natural life, and an order and a guiding law have been given to the functions of the body. For example, it is science which suggested maternal feeding, the abolition of swaddling clothes, baths, life in the open air, exercise, simple short clothing, quiet and plenty of sleep. Rules were also laid down for the measurement of food adapting it rationally to the physiological needs of the child's life.

Yet with all this, science made no contribution that was entirely new. Mothers had always nursed their children, children had always been clothed, they had breathed and eaten before.

The point is, that the same physical acts which, performed

blindly and without order, led to disease and death, when ordered *rationally* were the means of giving strength and life.

The great progress made may perhaps deceive us into thinking that everything possible has been done for children.

We have only to weigh the matter carefully, however, to reflect: Are our children only those healthy little bodies which today are growing and developing so vigorously under our eyes? Is their destiny fulfilled in the production of beautiful human bodies?

In that case there would be little difference between their lot and that of the animals which we raise that we may have good meat or beasts of burden.

Man's destiny is evidently other than this, and the care due to the child covers a field wider than that which is considered by physical hygiene. The mother who has given her child his bath and taken him in his carriage to the park has not fulfilled the mission of the "mother of humanity." The hen which gathers her chickens together, and the cat which licks her kittens and lavishes on them such tender care, differ in no wise from the human mother in the services they render.

No, the human mother if reduced to such limits devotes herself in vain, feels that a higher aspiration has been stifled within her. She is yet the mother of man.

Children must grow not only in the body but in the spirit, and the mother longs to follow the mysterious spiritual journey of the beloved one who tomorrow will be the intelligent, divine creation, man.

Science evidently has not finished its progress. On the contrary, it has scarcely taken the first step in advance, for it has hitherto stopped at the welfare of the body. It must continue, however, to advance; on the same positive lines along which it has improved the health and saved the physical life of the children, it is bound in the future to benefit and to reinforce their inner life, which is the real *human life.* On the same positive lines science will proceed to direct the development of the intelligence, of character, and of those latent creative forces which lie hidden in the marvelous embryo of man's spirit.

As the child's body must draw nourishment and oxygen from its external environment, in order to accomplish a great physiological work, the *work of growth,* so also the spirit must take from its environment the nourishment which it needs to develop according to its own "laws of growth." It cannot be denied that the phenomena of development are a great work in themselves. The consolidation of the bones, the growth of the whole body, the completion of the minute construction of the brain, the formation of the teeth, all these are very real labors of the physiological organism, as is also the transformation which the organism undergoes during the period of puberty.

These exertions are very different from those put forth by mankind in so-called *external work,* that is to say, in "social production," whether in the schools where man is taught, or in the world where, by the activity of his intelligence, he produces wealth and transforms his environment.

It is none the less true, however, that they are both "work." In fact, the organism during these periods of greatest physiological work is least capable of performing external tasks, and sometimes the work of growth is of such extent and difficulty that the individual is overburdened, as with an excessive strain, and for this reason alone becomes exhausted or even dies.

Man will always be able to avoid "external work" by making use of the labor of others, but there is no possibility of shirking that inner work. Together with birth and death it has been imposed by nature itself, and each man must accomplish it for himself. The difficult, inevitable labor, this is the "work of the child."

When we say then that little children should *rest* we are

referring to one side only of the question of work. We mean that they should rest from that *external* visible work to which the little child through his weakness and incapacity cannot make any contribution useful either to himself or to others.

Our assertion, therefore, is not absolute; the child in reality is not resting, he is performing the mysterious inner work of his autoformation. He is working to make a man, and to accomplish this it is not enough that the child's body should grow in actual size; the most intimate functions of the motor and nervous systems must also be established and the intelligence developed.

The functions to be established by the child fall into two groups: (1) the motor functions by which he is to secure his balance and learn to walk, and to coordinate his movements; (2) the sensory functions through which, receiving sensations from his environment, he lays the foundations of his intelligence by a continual exercise of observation, comparison and judgment. In this way he gradually comes to be acquainted with his environment and to develop his intelligence.

At the same time he is learning a *language,* and he is faced not only with the motor difficulties of articulation, sounds and words, but also with the difficulty of gaining an intelligent understanding of names and of the syntactical composition of the language.

If we think of an emigrant who goes to a new country ignorant of its products, ignorant of its natural appearance and social order, entirely ignorant of its language, we realize that there is an immense work of adaptation which he must perform before he can associate himself with the active life of the unknown people. No one will be able to do for him that work of adaptation. He himself must observe, understand, remember, form judgments, and learn the new language by laborious exercise and long experience.

What is to be said then of the child? What of this emigrant who comes into a new world, who, weak as he is and before his organism is completely developed, *must* in a short time adapt himself to a world so complex?

Up to the present day the little child has not received rational aid in the accomplishment of this laborious task. As regards the psychological development of the child we find ourselves in a period parallel to that in which the physical life was left to the mercy of chance and instinct—the period in which infant mortality was a scourge.

It is by scientific and rational means also that we must facilitate that inner work of psychological adaptation to be accomplished within the child, a work which is by no means the same thing as "any external work or production whatsoever."

This is the aim which underlies my method of infant education, and it is for this reason that certain principles which it enunciates, together with that part which deals with the technique of their practical application, are not of a general character, but have special reference to the particular case of the child from three to seven years of age, *i.e.*, to the needs of a formative period of life.

My method is scientific, both in its substance and in its aim. It makes for the attainment of a more advanced stage of progress, in directions no longer only material and physiological. It is an endeavor to complete the course which hygiene has already taken, but in the treatment of the physical side alone.

If today we possessed statistics respecting the nervous debility, defects of speech, errors of perception and of reasoning, and lack of character in normal children, it would perhaps be interesting to compare them with statistics of the same nature, but compiled from the study of children who have had a number of years of rational education. In all probability we should find a striking resemblance between such statistics and those today available showing the decrease in mortality and the improvement in the physical development of children.

Implications of Montessori's
Message—A Review

W HAT are some of the implications for the American educational establishment of the message in Dr. Montessori's *Handbook*?

If research continues to bear out the validity of Montessori's approach to early childhood education, and there is good reason to believe that it will, then our educational system must indeed undergo a revolution. In fact, evidence is accumulating which indicates that the beginnings of such a revolution are already underway. Much of this evidence has been cited in the *Handbook*.

Montessori speaks of the need to implement an "education from birth" for all children, an education conceived broadly as an aid to child development. The child's absorbent mind, sensitive periods, and formative period are all manifestations of an inner power that must be utilized during the child's early years. Every child must be given a systematic and sequential preparation for, and programmed experience in, sensory motor and cognitive learning, leading to self-mastery and mastery of the environment. Language, in the broad sense of neurological codes derived from experiential patterns, must be thoroughly developed. Childhood is the age for learning one's mother tongue well, and a second language.

Every child, then, needs a prepared environment in which the materials and methodology of auto-education free his potential to absorb and to ultimately improve upon the best of our cultural, social and ethical heritage. Contemporary educational assumptions and practices must undergo evaluation and modification where indicated. Long-cherished ideas about timing, curriculum, learning format, grade structure and schedules, motivation, rating of student performance, and teacher training must be reappraised in the light of past and present successful results with the Montessori Method.

Montessori, for example, recommends that children should be initially exposed to a prepared environment of learning not at age five or six, but at age two or three. She also points out that an age range of at least three years within a class enhances the learning situation. Children should not be grouped together merely because they are chronologically, say, six years of age. Montessori's practice of having a three-year age span within a class, with freedom of movement between classes, antecedes current interest in the "non-graded elementary school" or "ungraded primary." In the organization of such a school, described by educators John Goodlad and Robert Anderson,[1] arbitrary grade barriers are eliminated to permit greater flexibility of pupil movement. Long blocks of uninterrupted time necessary for the child's concentration must replace artificial periods composed of an inflexible number of minutes. The rigid scheduling found in many elementary schools is, of course, largely an administrative convenience.

The child who is experiencing the joy of work and discovery in a "Children's House" has little need for extrinsic prizes. In the new education, "auto-evaluation" makes teacher-imposed grades unnecessary. The satisfaction of self-development replaces the gold star. Finally, teacher education must be restructured on proven Montessori principles, with emphasis upon the teacher's role of observer. As she becomes more experimental and less expository, many of the traditional teacher's notions about the nature of intelligence, testing, motivation, communication, and other factors operating in the learning process may well have to change.

Montessori sees the teacher as a guide and guardian—a guardian of the environment and of the child's inalienable right to learn. She is the authoritative presence who can also function as the authoritarian where required, intervening directly and even forcefully if necessary on certain occasions, as when a child exceeds the limits of allowable behavior. The Montessori teacher, then, is not an inert nonparticipant in the "prepared environment," nor do the children in such an environment evolve a general concensus as to what they are to learn. Rather, the children are exposed to a sequence of learning that has already been carefully thought out by the teacher, in relation to what the culture will expect of the children.

The teacher's role in presenting this sequence, so that mastery of simpler tasks by the child leads to more difficult ones, makes of her what could be termed in modern parlance a "programmer." To the extent that a teacher is one who takes a thoroughly active part in the learning process, a Montessorian is no different from any other well-organized teacher. However, the Montessorian characteristically takes an active part in the learning process not by implicating herself in it, but by disposing the child to achievement, to success. By means of her actions as a "programmer," she enables the child to move from one task to the next with confidence and competence, building at each level on what has gone before and anticipating what will come next.

The rationale of the Montessori "didactic apparatus" is in many ways analogous to the more recent notion of "programmed learning," involving the development of sequences of factual material that can be utilized by an individual learner at his own pace. The Montessori material, like modern programmed material, is designed to place the child in direct contact with content. The programmed sequence of both furnishes the pacing that verbal stimuli of the teacher would ordinarily provide, thereby eliminating the need for direct intervention by the teacher in the child's actual learning process.

But, once again, this is not to say that the Montessori teacher withdraws from any kind of interpersonal contact with the children, from any kind of group instruction or personal intrusion, as it were, on the learning process where such is required. Providing for the needs of the individual learner within the context of the group is a pedagogical goal to which traditional education has probably always given at least lip service, but it is only in relatively recent years that genuine individualization has become practical, methodologically. Today, such innovations as the structured nursery, language laboratories, the ungraded primary, and teaching machines promise a new dimension of "auto-education," as Montessori termed it, for our public schools.

Miss Anne E. George was Dr. Montessori's first American pupil, and the first teacher to apply the Montessori method in America. Professor Earl Barnes, having visited Miss George's Montessori school, wrote that Dr. Montessori has brought us "a reinterpretation of the whole educational process." Few educators have done as much. But Montessori has left us an even more important legacy—a reinterpretation of human nature. The supreme merit of the Montessori method, as Edmond Holmes has aptly put it, is that it is based on "trust in human nature."

Is it not time for us to implement that trust?

R. C. OREM

Selected References

[1] Goodlad, John and Robert Anderson, *The Nongraded Elementary School.* New York: Harcourt, Brace & World. Revised Edition, 1963.

Appendices

1

A Guide to the Essential
Features of a Good
Montessori School

INTEREST in early childhood education is rapidly increasing in America. Current research in the psychology of learning and related fields is demonstrating the crucial importance of the years from birth to age six, the formative period when patterns and "sets" for subsequent learning and behavior are established. We know, for example, that the child absorbs language most readily during his formative years. He should likewise be given preparation for mathematics, science, writing, reading, and other skills at this time. It must be emphasized that a stimulating environment is essential to the child's full physical, psychological, intellectual, and social development.

With the increased interest in early childhood education has come a mounting interest in the Montessori Method specifically. Although much study is still to be done, the basic principles of the Montessori Method are proving to be in harmony with recent findings in the behavioral sciences. Many investigators (J. McV. Hunt, William Fowler, L. K. Frank, and W. Grey Walter, to name but a few) have been pointing out the possibilities of the Montessori techniques and materials.

One outcome of the unabated interest in Montessori has been the demand by parents for schools employing her approach. To meet this demand, an ever-increasing number of schools that directly or indirectly claim to utilize the Montessori approach has been opening, and there is every indication that the number of Montessori schools will increase greatly in the near future. This trend, in turn, has created a heavy demand for Montessori teachers. Various American Montessori teacher-training courses are now being held or are in the planning stages. In some cases, administrators have been able to obtain qualified teachers from England, India, and other countries.

Parents are naturally interested in what makes a "good" Montessori school. Of special concern to them are the criteria by which an effective Montessori teacher may be identified. What are the qualities which mark her as a Montessorian? Because the name "Montessori" cannot be copyrighted, schools are free to use it in various ways; moreover, Montessori teacher training is not as yet uniform, and such training must be closely evaluated. Some nursery schools currently claim to be utilizing "the best of Montessori," without specifying precisely what this "best" is. Some teachers are labeled "trained in Montessori" on the basis of attendance at a summer institute or a series of lectures. Parents faced with all kinds of Montessori schools, employing teachers with varying amounts of formal and informal training, wonder how to determine the authenticity of a particular school. Parents in such a situation may find the following guide helpful. It is organized in terms of five topics: Philosophy, Personnel, Plant, Program, and Pupils.

Philosophy: Schools, like all institutions, operate from some kind of philosophical base. This base includes the goals and functions of the school. Dr. Maria Montessori's philosophy is found in her books, *The Montessori Method, The Advanced Montessori Method,*[1] and *The Absorbent Mind.*[2]

Parents, after reading as much of Montessori's work as they need to understand her position on various educational issues, should then compare her philosophy with that of the school in question. This can be done by reading literature about the school, by observation, and by talking with the staff. The question then remains: "What does the staff really believe and practice?"

Personnel: Parents should ascertain the type and amount of formal Montessori training that the prospective teacher of their child has had, in addition to her general educational background. This would include length and content of Montessori courses, where given, by whom taught, under whose auspices, and extent of practical work and internship. The question for the parent is now: "Is the teacher qualified as a Montessorian by training?"

Parents should also know the amount and quality of experience that the teacher has had with young children, including Americans. The question here becomes: "Is the teacher qualified as a Montessorian by experience?" Finally, parents will want to know the teacher as a person. Is she the kind of person who can form empathic human relationships? The parent will ask here: "Is the development of the teacher's personality such that she can foster the optimum development of my child?"

Plant: In addition to meeting basic health, safety, zoning, and other standards, the Montessori school must offer the "best for the child" in a prepared environment. This includes ample space and equipment for outdoor activities such as gardening and gymnastics. Furnishings should include chairs and tables designed for children, and carpets for work at floor level. The exercises of practical life requires a child-sized sink and functional housekeeping equipment.

A complete set of Montessori didactic apparatus kept in excellent condition is essential, supplemented with appropriate books, models, word games, etc. The question here is:

"Does the school represent in reality a 'Children's House,' with all the materials necessary for muscular, sensory, and language education?"

Program: Parents should visit classes to watch the children at work, there being no excuse for a "closed-door" policy in a Montessori school. A balance of individual and group activities should be in evidence, with children free much of the time to work alone on self-selected tasks at their own pace. As the children move about purposefully in self-disciplined fashion, the teacher will be giving many individual lessons. The question for the parent here is: "Are the children engaged in 'auto-education' within an atmosphere of 'liberty within limits,' leading to mastery of themselves and of the environment?"

Pupils: The proof of the method (and of the school) is in the children. The Montessori child should demonstrate by his actions an increasing competence in the areas of physical, psychological, intellectual, and social development. This includes the following: muscular coordination and care of his person; accurate perception of his world; ability to concentrate upon and complete meaningful tasks; effective communication; preparation for and proficiency in mathematics and science; manners showing respect for the rights of others, and growth of inner direction. The ultimate question is: "Are the children achieving ever-higher levels of independence?"

These five topics, then, serve as a general framework against which parents may evaluate a school in terms of its Montessori components. If, in a particular school, (a) the staff really believes and practices Montessori principles, (b) the teachers are qualified Montessorians by dint of proper training, (c) there are all the facilities and equipment necessary for a prepared environment, (d) the orientation is "auto-education," and (e) the pupils are achieving ever-higher levels of perception, communication, cognition, creativity, and self-direction, then that school is truly a Montessori one. Conversely, to the degree that a school lacks (a) Montessori philosophy and practice, (b) qualified Montessori teachers, (c) Montessori didactic apparatus, (d) Montessori "auto-education" and curriculum, and (e) pupils working toward mastery of themselves and their environment, then, to that degree, the school is surely not a Montessori one.

GENEVIEVE TARLTON ALEXANDER, WITH R. C. OREM

Selected References

[1] Montessori, Maria, *The Montessori Method,* New York, Frederick Stokes, 1912; and *The Advanced Montessori Method:* Vol. I, *Spontaneous Activity in Education;* Vol. II, *The Montessori Elementary Material,* New York. Frederick Stokes, 1917. These works have been reprinted in cloth and paperback editions.

[2] Montessori, Maria, *The Absorbent Mind.* Adyar, Madras 20, India: The Theosophical Publishing House, Third Edition, 1961.

INDEX OF SPECIFIC ELEMENTS AND ASPECTS OF THE MONTESSORI METHOD IN *DR. MONTESSORI'S OWN HANDBOOK*

In place of a formal index, the editor has prepared the following list of specific elements and aspects of the Montessori Method that can be found in the text of *Dr. Montessori's Own Handbook.* They are given here in the sequence in which they appear in this revised edition of the *Handbook.* The brief wording of each of these elements or aspects is intended as a paraphrase of a noteworthy point made by Montessori. It is hoped that this index will serve as a useful guide to the *Handbook,* as well as to the Montessori Method itself.

I. THE MONTESSORI STRUCTURE

A "CHILDREN'S HOUSE"
  Casa dei Bambini as a prepared environment
  "Children's House" flexible in design
  "Children's House," not a play house
  Much activity outdoors

Provision for intellectual work is central
Other specialized rooms when possible
Environment adapted to child's needs
Functional child-sized furniture
A place for everything
Attractive and educational decor
Utilization of carpeted floor as work space
The best for the child
Learning with genuine utensils
Opportunity for care of environment and person
Reality-oriented education

OUTLINE OF METHOD AND MATERIALS
A three-part methodology
Didactic material for education of the senses
Didactic material for the preparation for writing and
    arithmetic

FREEDOM
Teacher as guide
Teacher's attitude crucial
The self-directed "normalized" child
Teacher as patient observer
Child needs respect as well as adult
Adults mistreat child
Kindness as consisting of respectful service to child
Scientific study of child to determine his needs
Aid child indirectly by providing him opportunity for
    self-development
Observe child developing in freedom
Child prepared for conquests
Normalized personality emerging in prepared en-
    vironment
Feeling of responsibility developed
Functional order
Didactic exercises lead to ordered mind
Auto-formation
Child educated for ordered observation

II. THE IMPORTANCE OF MOVEMENT IN EDUCATION

MOTOR EDUCATION

THE MONTESSORI PEDOMETER

Children care for Pedometer
Importance of measurement in scientific pedagogy

III. SENSORY EDUCATION AND MUSIC

SENSORY EDUCATION
The solid insets
Programmed difficulty in materials
Child in direct contact with real objects
Nonintervention or artful intervention
"Control of error" in materials provides learner with
"feedback"
Young child's love of repetition
Didactic materials must interest the child
Training for observation
Auto-correction
Auto-education intrinsically motivated
The pink cubes—variation in size (from large to small)
The quadrilateral prisms—variation in thickness (from thick to thin)
The colored rods—variation in length (from long to short)
Children learn from each other—"child as teacher"
Teacher as observer
The "value of error"
The joy of discovery
Training for visual perception of dimension
Importance of preparation
Education of the tactile sense important
Intervention by teacher when necessary
Perfection through practice with increasingly similar stimuli
Training in stereognostic feeling
Isolating the senses—blindfolding
Exploring the environment
The color materials for education of the chromatic sense
Exercises in pairing the colors

Prepared mind of scientist

Scientist's training in observation and classification as preparation for discovery

Montessori children prepared for joy of discovery

WRITING

Language, by "fixing ideas," facilitates ordering of mind

Child as explorer

Children prepared for writing and arithmetic

Children prepared for "cultural input"

"Fixing" function of arithmetic and writing

The hand prepared for writing

Two-phased direct preparation for writing

Didactic material for the management of the instrument of writing

Development of didactic material through long trial

Use of the metal insets

Tracing an outline of the geometric forms

Tracing the second outline

Importance of attention to details in Montessori pedagogy

Filling in the traced form

Practice for precision

Attention span of child not short

Filling in prepared designs

Child's freedom of choice

Free children reveal new characteristics

Drawings provide limits for a purpose

Maximum utilization of educational situation

Didactic material for writing alphabetical signs

Touching the sandpaper letters

Importance of motor preparation for writing

Multisensory approach to learning

Concurrent preparation for writing and reading

Mastery of sub-tasks leading to synthesis

Using the movable alphabet

Two movable alphabets

Explosion into writing

"Naughtiness" disappears when child is free to develop

Joy of work, learning, and discovery replaces rage

Child struggles for defense of psychic integrity

Personality expansion in psychically hygienic environment

Universal need for care of developing child

Physical nourishment important, but only one factor

Need for mental hygiene

Organization of work, and liberty essential for child's optimum development

Interdependence of organization of work and liberty

Civilization founded upon organization of work and liberty

Child as hope of mankind

Remove obstacles to child's development

THE NEW EDUCATION

Century of the child

Emergent man

Science of child care

Science in the service of nature

Man's destiny unfulfilled

Mother's mission unfulfilled

Physical hygiene not sufficient

Hygiene of spirit needed

Physiological work of child

Adult's work external

Internal work requires environmental care

Child's work inevitable

Child as maker of man

Child's motor and sensory functions

Language function

Adaptability of child

Facilitation of child's inner work required

Serving the formative period

Montessori Method scientific

Rational education to decrease psychological maladies

THE EDITOR

R. C. OREM, M.Ed., a former public and private school teacher and educational specialist with the Department of Defense, is presently an administrator at the Washington, D.C., Children's Center. He has written and lectured extensively on such subjects as the Montessori Method, reading techniques and early childhood education.

THE CONTRIBUTORS

GENEVIEVE TARLTON ALEXANDER, M.A., a former public school teacher and university instructor, is the founder and headmistress of the Lilliput Schoolhouse, the first Montessori school in Corpus Christi, Texas. Mrs. Alexander also conducts lectures and seminars on Montessori throughout the Southwest.

WILLIAM E. AMOS, M.A., M.Ed., Ed.D., a certified school psychologist and a former high school principal and public school superintendent, is now Chief, Division of Youth Employment and Guidance Services of the U. S. Employment Service, and a lecturer at the George Washington University.

E. PAUL BENOIT, M.A., Ph.D., Director of the Jewish Foundation for Retarded Children, is a clinical psychologist. He holds staff appointments at Georgetown University Medical School, the University of Virginia, and the Catholic University. Consultant to the National Committee for Children and Youth, the American Psychiatric Association, and the Alfred Adler Mental Hygiene Clinic, he has published some fifty articles on educational programming and on various philosophical and scientific implications of mental retardation, a field in which he has been active for over 17 years.

GERTRUDE R. JUSTISON, B.S., R.N., M.A., Ed.D., F.A.A.M.D., is former Assistant Dean of the Georgetown University School of Nursing. A teacher, elementary school principal, assistant supervisor of special education, and college instructor, she is currently teaching special education at Howard University.

NEIL D. KOPPENHAVER, B.S., M.A., Ph.D., has been a clinical psychologist with the Veterans Administration and consulting psychologist at the Laboratory of Psychological Studies, Stevens Institute of Technology. He is now Assistant Chief, Psychology Services at the D.C. Government Children's Center, where his duties include conducting and supervising individual and group psychotherapy and counseling with delinquent boys and girls.

PAUL LEWIS, O.D., conducts a child-centered practice of Optometry in Silver Spring, Maryland, and is Director of the Maryland Chapter of the Optometric Extension Program. He serves as optometric consultant to the University of Maryland Physical Development Clinic, the Syracuse University Department of Special Education, and the Boards of Education of Montgomery County and Prince Georges County, Maryland.

ELIZABETH JANE OLIVERIA, M.D., is a graduate of the Tulane Medical School. For the past five years she has been engaged in general practice in Corpus Christi, Texas, where she is medical consultant to the Lilliput Schoolhouse, the Montessori school attended by her three children.

JO ANN T. REDDIT, B.F.A., a former art teacher, is now a commercial artist by profession. She has been a leader in Montessori study groups for a number of years, and her two children attend a Montessori school.

GEORGE L. STEVENS, Ph.B., M.A., is director of Reading Technics, a private consulting firm that provides reading and writing improvement programs for industry, education, and government, including the National Institutes of Health and the Department of the Army. A provocative writer on the subject of the teaching of reading, he is on the board of the Seton Montessori School (Virginia) and has participated in several major Montessori seminars.